Diary of an [extra]ORDINARY woman

Text copyright © Clare Blake 2006
The author asserts the moral right
to be identified as the author of this work

Published by
The Bible Reading Fellowship
First Floor, Elsfield Hall
15–17 Elsfield Way, Oxford OX2 8FG
Website: www.brf.org.uk

ISBN 1 84101 426 5
13-digit ISBN 978 1 84101 426 5
First published 2006
10 9 8 7 6 5 4 3 2 1 0
All rights reserved

Acknowledgments
Unless otherwise stated, scripture quotations are taken from the Holy Bible, New International Version, copyright © 1973, 1978, 1984 by International Bible Society, and are used by permission of Hodder & Stoughton Limited. All rights reserved. 'NIV' is a registered trademark of International Bible Society. UK trademark number 1448790.

Scripture quotations taken from The New Revised Standard Version of the Bible, Anglicized Edition, copyright © 1989, 1995 by the Division of Christian Education of the National Council of the Churches of Christ in the USA, are used by permission. All rights reserved.

Extracts from the Authorized Version of the Bible (The King James Bible), the rights in which are vested in the Crown, are reproduced by permission of the Crown's patentee, Cambridge University Press.

A catalogue record for this book is available from the British Library

Printed in Singapore by Craft Print International Ltd

Diary of an [extra]ORDINARY woman

CLARE blake

Learning to listen to God day by day

*To three much-loved sisters
Hilary, Helen, and Celia*

Acknowledgments

Writing a book is very much like having a baby—sometimes it seems as though the day of its birth will never come! Thanks are due to my 'spiritual midwives' who were a source of real help and encouragement—to Naomi and the team at BRF, to my home church, Exeter Frontiers, to the 'pray-ers', Wendy, Sheila, Laurie and many others, to writing friends for constant stimulation, and to my family who shared the load and provided much of the subject matter. Thanks for the love and fun we share!

Most of all, of course, I want to thank my heavenly Father, without whom this book would just be so many blank pages—your love is amazing!

Contents

Prologue 6

New Year 7

Spring 15

Summer 51

Autumn 85

Winter 121

Prologue

Hands up if you're perfect. No? What a relief, neither am I! Superstars we ain't, but we are women who want to live for God.

Of course, it's not easy, and sometimes we get stuck. When I was learning to swim, the swimming instructor used to shout, 'For goodness' sake, take your feet off the bottom!'

Sometimes, it's like that in our Christian life. We want to keep at least one of our toes on solid ground because we're scared of getting out of our depth, but it's impossible to learn to swim that way.

Our feelings let us down, telling us that this is not for us—we're never going to be good swimmers—never going to do much for God. But God is the perfect craftsman, and he made you! He is perfect and so is his handiwork.

God takes the ordinary and makes it extraordinary, and that is exactly what happens to us when we give our lives into his hands—we are no longer ordinary women but *extraordinary* women. Trusting in him, we no longer try to keep our toes touching the bottom, but gain the confidence to swim further and more strongly than we have ever done before.

Have you taken the plunge yet?

NEW YEAR

This is the day the Lord has made;
let us rejoice and be glad in it.
PSALM 118:24

I said,
'Take my hands'
but when Father asked,
'Do this, my child,'
I said I had
some other thing in mind,
the Really Important Thing
I'm going to do for God
one of these days.
It's only a matter of time,
and of course right now
I'm still waiting and praying,
considering all the options.
It hasn't arrived yet
but I'll know it when I see it…

It's just that right now
I'm awfully busy,
things seem to be getting
on top of me lately
you know how it is.
And God, I can say this
because you still love me whatever I do,
but…
would it be OK if you came back
when it was a little more convenient,
when of course I'll be only too pleased
to listen to more of your suggestions?
Just
Not
Right
Now.

31 December

Steve taps on the bathroom door. 'We'll be going in another twenty minutes.'

'I'm almost ready,' I call back.

I go into our bedroom, and take my favourite blue dress out of the wardrobe. It's party time, and I want to look my best.

I start to put it on, but something very odd seems to have happened. It seems to be a much tighter squeeze than I remembered, and the material is stretching in rather an ominous way.

I start to do up the buttons, but to my surprise they don't quite meet in some places. I tug gently at the material—it must be slightly crooked. If I straighten it, there won't be a problem.

I take a deep breath and finish doing up the buttons. That's better—I knew it was just a matter of readjustment.

Unfortunately, I can't hold my breath for ever. I let the air out, and the dress material tightens again. It's a bit like wearing a very pretty straitjacket. I have almost no freedom of movement at all. Surely the dress can't have shrunk—I always wash it so carefully.

I walk stiffly over to the mirror, and look at myself. Instead of flattering my shape, the dress exaggerates every imperfection.

'It's too tight!' I wail.

'What's the matter?' Steve appears in the doorway, a frown of concern on his face.

'Look,' I say, turning round to face him.

'That looks fabulous.'

I glare at him.

'Doesn't it?'

'No.' I try to pull the material smooth.

'Oh, I see what you mean. It is a bit…'

'Don't say it...'
'Well-fitting.'
I slump down on to the bed.
'I can't wear this. I'll have to wear something else.'

I can't believe it. My body's played a trick on me when I wasn't looking. That isn't me in the mirror.

Earlier in the day I'd met up with friends, and we'd jokingly jotted down some New Year resolutions for the year ahead. Mentally, I add a new one in big letters at the top of the list:

'GO ON A DIET!'

❖

New Year is traditionally the time for looking at changes we could make in our lives.

- Be nicer to my husband/boyfriend/flatmate.
- Eat less chocolate.
- Stand up for myself more at work.
- Pray and read my Bible *every* day.

There's something in us that loves the idea of a fresh start.

Remember the excitement of getting a new exercise book at school, full of blank pages that have yet to be written on? For the first few sheets you use your best handwriting, and every diagram is inked in with the greatest care, but turn over a few more pages and it's back to normal, with crossings out and untidy scrawls.

So many people look back on their lives and say, 'If I could have my life over again, I'd do it all so differently.' We love the idea of being able to reinvent ourselves, to be the 'nice' person we always wanted to be.

Sadly, New Year resolutions, together with all our other efforts to change ourselves, tend to be short-lived in spite of our good intentions. We just can't seem to keep it up.

God is intensely interested in new beginnings and fresh starts of a more permanent kind. Indeed, he specializes in them, however unpromising the material may appear.

Just look at Simon, a fisherman from Galilee. There's no doubt that he's good at what he does. Simon knows everything there is to know about catching fish. His days are made up of mending nets in preparation for putting out to sea to fish, and then returning home with a big catch. It's a satisfying job, and Simon wants no other. It suits him just fine.

But all that is about to change. One morning, Simon is washing his nets, tired and fed up from a long night when he has caught nothing (Luke 5:1–11). He might as well have stayed at home. What a waste of time!

As he washes the nets, a man called Jesus asks if he can sit in Simon's boat to speak to the crowd following him. Simon agrees—there's something different about this man, and he's curious to know more.

He listens as the man speaks, feeling his heart strangely warmed. What is it? Why does he feel like this?

When Jesus finishes, he turns to Simon. Simon thinks he's going to say something more on what he's just been talking about, but he doesn't. To Simon's annoyance, Jesus is giving him, the professional fisherman, fishing advice. 'Put out into the deep water and let down your nets for a catch.'

Simon wants to protest—loudly! He's always been known for speaking his mind. 'Hang on a minute, Jesus. Fishing is my trade, not yours. You're a carpenter, remember. I've already been out there all night, and I'm willing to stake my life that there are no fish. I just want to go to bed.'

Uncharacteristically, however, he says nothing. He knows if he does what Jesus asks, he's going to look a complete fool in front of the other fishermen. What will they say when they see him lowering his nets? They all know it's a pointless activity. None of them has caught so much as a sprat. But he can't turn Jesus down either. What is it about this man?

In the end, Simon compromises, making it absolutely clear that it's all Jesus' idea, and goes against his better judgment. 'Master, we have worked all night long but caught nothing. Yet if you say so, I will let down the nets.'

Reluctantly, Simon sails back into the deeper waters. 'I don't know why I'm doing this,' he mutters to himself as he lowers the nets once more. How long must he wait before he can turn back to shore? Half an hour should be enough to satisfy Jesus, surely.

But within minutes the nets are heaving. Simon rubs his eyes in disbelief—a catch, and such a catch! The nets are beginning to break under the weight of shining fish, and another boat has to come over to help.

Simon is completely humbled. He knows about fish, and he knows that what has just happened is impossible. Totally broken, he kneels at Jesus' feet. 'Go away from me, Lord, for I am a sinful man.'

Simon thought he knew exactly where his life was headed—he would fish until he could fish no more—but Jesus had something different in store for him. The old fisherman clothes do not fit any more. From now on he will 'catch people'. Even his name will change. He will become known as Peter, the rock.

Romans 6:4 tells us that Christ was raised from the dead so that 'we too may live a new life'. Tempting though it is to hang on to our old lifestyles, we too have to learn to walk away. You cannot put new wine in old wineskins or they will split; you cannot put a new patch on an old garment or the material will pull away (Luke 5:36–38). Only something completely new will do.

New Year resolutions only offer us the opportunity to make a fresh start once a year, but for Christians, God's grace is freely available whenever we need it.

The steadfast love of the Lord never ceases,
his mercies never come to an end;
they are new every morning.
LAMENTATIONS 3:22–23 (NRSV)

Walking in newness of life is an ongoing process. When we first met God, he changed our lives for ever, but it didn't stop there. Each brand new day, as we walk with him, he still does.

SPRING

Forget the former things;
do not dwell on the past.
See, I am doing a new thing!
Now it springs up; do you not perceive it?
ISAIAH 43:18–19

2 March

Moving to the city has meant a bigger mortgage, and, looking in my purse, I discover it's going to require some budgeting to cater for hearty teenage appetites and provide nourishing meals for the family this week.

I park the supermarket trolley to one side where it won't get in people's way, and I'm bending down to read the price labels on the tins on the bottom shelf. Which is best value for money? Should I go for the largest size and cook a meal that will last two days? Unlikely in my family! It doesn't seem to matter how much is in the dish, you can guarantee it will be scraped clean at the end of the meal.

There's a tap on my shoulder. I look around expecting to see someone I know, but it's a little old lady. She points to the tin in my hand. 'How much are those, dear?'

I tell her. She shakes her head. 'I think they're a bit too large for me. What about those?' She points to a smaller tin on the second shelf. I get it down for her and, after careful consideration, she pops it into her basket.

'Thank you, my dear. You've been most helpful. Now, I know they have a scheme to reward good employees.'

'But I'm not…' I start to protest.

'Nonsense, dear. I know you're only doing your job, but I believe politeness and friendliness shouldn't go unnoticed, don't you?'

I nod weakly.

She totters off in the direction of a nearby supervisor, and I take my trolley and skulk down the opposite aisle, although that doesn't prevent me from hearing, 'What lovely helpful staff you have here!'

Half of me wants to laugh, half of me feels slightly offended at being mistaken for a member of the supermarket staff. What does that say about my dress sense?!

✧

Mistaken identity is something that happens all the time. It can be funny, annoying or even embarrassing. I still remember a time when I was out shopping with Steve and caught hold of what I thought was his hand, only to find that it actually belonged to someone completely different. 'I thought you were my husband,' I stuttered. He looked more than a little worried!

Jesus was frequently mistaken for someone other than who he really was. In fact, in his home town he was unable to do many works of power, because the people thought they knew exactly who he was already. 'Isn't this the carpenter's son? Isn't his mother's name Mary, and aren't his brothers James, Joseph, Simon and Judas? Aren't all his sisters with us? Where then did this man get all these things?' (Matthew 13:55–56).

For the scribes and Pharisees, the religious leaders of the day, Jesus posed enormous problems. How could he be the Messiah when he was clearly a glutton and a drunkard, a friend of tax collectors and sinners (Matthew 11:19)? No, in their view, the man was a dangerous heretic and blasphemer, leading the crowds astray, and the sooner he was removed from the scene, the better.

Even people who should have known better seemed to need reassurance about Jesus' identity. John the Baptist sent his disciples to ask Jesus, 'Are you the one who was to come, or should we expect someone else?' (Matthew 11:3).

Interestingly, Jesus never felt the need to trumpet his own credentials. He let his actions and words speak for themselves.

When Jesus asked his disciples, 'Who do you say I am?' Peter had no hesitation. 'You are the Messiah, the Son of the living God' (Matthew 16:15–16).

Today, we are equally surrounded by people who are confused about the identity of Jesus. Is Jesus:

- a good man?
- an influential leader?

- a wise teacher?
- a fantasy Santa Claus-type figure?
- a crutch for losers?

Few seem to recognize him for who he really is—the Son of God.

What about us as Christians? Do we sometimes lose sight of who Jesus really is? Do you know who you believe in?

Sometimes, it seems, we too can forget that Jesus is the Son of God. We treat him like a slot machine. We put our prayer request in, and if we don't get the answer we want, we push him to one side.

When things go wrong, do we still trust that Jesus is Lord?

- When our job disappears?
- When our marriage is in problems?
- When finances are a burden?
- When family and friends disappoint us?

'Who do you say I am?' is a question that Jesus still asks of us today. What is our answer?

7 March

'So, what are you having?'

'I'm not quite ready to order yet.'

I peer at the menu. The candle on the table is a nice romantic touch, but at this moment I would prefer the brightness of a 100-watt electric bulb.

I've been moving the menu discreetly backwards and forwards for some time, hoping that my husband won't notice, but the words are still just a blur. I try squinting.

'Are you all right?' Steve asks, with concern.

Hastily, I unscrew my eyes. 'Yes, fine.'

I try for a few more minutes, but finally have to admit defeat. If I sat here for a hundred years, I still wouldn't be able to decipher the curving script, and I'm hungry.

'The light in here's a bit dim. Could you tell me what's on the menu?'

I pass it over. My husband takes it from me, and looks at it for a moment. Then he puts it down with a sigh. 'You know, you really do need glasses,' he says, not for the first time.

I know he's right. It's been creeping up on me for some time. At first it was just a case of needing to focus a little more carefully, but recently I've been really struggling. I've noticed that I can't see the words in the church songbook, or in my Bible, without real effort.

More than once our youngest son has seen me frowning as I've tried to make sense of the cooking instructions on the back of a packet, and taken pity on me. 'Here, Mum, let me look at it. Right… 20 minutes at Gas Mark 5.' So simple if you can only see it!

I've blamed my growing inability to see clearly on many things—tiredness, the smallness of the print, the amount of light in the room—but I know I've been fooling myself. It's time to face facts. My eyes are simply not as good as they once were. And I do need glasses.

Steve comes along with me for moral support when I go shopping for spectacles. It's just as well—if he hadn't come I think I might still have put it off, telling myself it really wasn't so bad that it needed dealing with quite yet. I could cope.

There are some sample lenses, and I try them one after the other, peering at what surely cannot be words—they look more like an untidy ink trail left by a spider.

When I prop the fourth pair of glasses on my nose, however, it's like a minor miracle. I can read what it says on the card! I probably haven't been as excited as this since I first learned to read and discovered what the word shapes meant.

'I can see!' I announce proudly.

✛

If only it could be as easy when we seem to be groping along in total darkness at certain stages of our lives.

'Where is God? What on earth is he doing? What's happening to me?' Cries of pain, frustration and fear. We don't understand what's happening, and we feel as though we are shut behind a door in a darkened room where there is no trace of light.

Perhaps we are undergoing serious trauma of some kind—severe illness, bereavement or broken relationships—and don't know where to turn. And we cry out in our loneliness, fearing that we have been abandoned because we cannot sense God's presence in what is happening to us.

'I just can't see God's hand in this!' we cry out in despair.

It is hard when we cannot see clearly, when our vision fails us.

Elisha's servant was terrified (2 Kings 6:8–17). With God's help, the prophet Elisha had warned the king of Israel many times when danger threatened, but now Israel's enemy, the king of Aram, had decided that the man of God would pay dearly for his interference.

Now, everywhere Elisha's frightened servant looked, there were enemy soldiers. The hostile army with its horses and chariots had totally surrounded the city, cutting off any escape route. Surely they were trapped, and would now die. 'Oh, my lord, what shall we do?' he cried (v. 15).

It seemed there was no way out. They had no army to protect them, and Elisha didn't have any weapons. The situation was surely a desperate one... or was it?

Elisha's servant looked with his human vision, and all he could see was imminent disaster.

Elisha saw exactly the same scenario, but something else too.

He encouraged the terrified man, 'Don't be afraid... Those who are with us are more than those who are with them' (v. 16).

For a moment the servant's spirits lifted. Had the king of Israel come to their rescue? But he could see nobody except the two of them. His poor master—obviously the whole thing had been too much for him.

Elisha then prayed very simply, 'O Lord, open his eyes so he may see' (v. 17).

Then the frightened man finally saw for himself what Elisha had been able to see all along—the situation as it really was. The servant had thought they were totally on their own, hopelessly outnumbered, and facing certain disaster, but in an instant his whole viewpoint changed.

From his new perspective, he could laugh at his former fears. Who could be afraid of the army of the king of Aram now? It didn't stand a chance. The whole mountain was full of horses and chariots of fire all around Elisha and his servant.

How good is our vision when we find ourselves in a difficult situation?

Do we rely on human perception, like Elisha's servant, prone to a lack of clarity that often leads us to conclude despairingly, 'There's no way out'?

Or do we use godly vision like Elisha who saw the threat of the enemy army from a completely different perspective?

As the prophet's servant learned, appearances can be very deceptive. When we are overwhelmed, are we able to see God's presence in what we are facing? Do we need an adjustment to our vision?

Sometimes we need to pray for our blindness to be lifted, for the blurring that is causing us to be disorientated and confused to clear. Only then will we see God's hand in what is going on, in the pain, the sweat and the tears.

'O Lord, help us not to be blind, but to see you in every situation, however bad it appears, however hopeless—to know that whatever trouble we face, we do not face it alone, for you are here right beside us.'

'Don't be afraid… Those who are with us are more than those who are with them.'

We are on the winning side.

12 March

Our church is singing in the town centre today. It's raining, so we have our umbrellas up. 'Good,' whispers Carol. 'There won't be so many people out and about.' I know what she means.

Our church banner gets soggier by the minute, but we gather round it as Simon prays simply that what we sing will touch the hearts of those passing by—even if we aren't always in tune!

We shuffle our feet and prepare to sing, not knowing quite where to look. I see a young mother passing with two children. Our eyes meet and I smile, but have the feeling that it looks fake, like a toothpaste advertisement. She pulls up her collar and almost drags the two children away. Hmm... not a very promising beginning.

Carol and I are sharing a song sheet, but I've forgotten my glasses and can't see the words. However, that doesn't stop me seeing a neighbour from our road doing a quick double-take as she spots me. I see her nudge her husband and they both stop.

Trying to look as though this is something I do every day—and no, of course I'm not embarrassed, not at all—I go over to chat for a few minutes.

'So you're doing this with your church?' (Slightly raised eyebrows.)

Her husband joins in heartily, 'Well, pass the collection box, and we'll put something in.'

'We're not collecting for anything,' I explain.

Not collecting. Just singing. In the street.

You can almost read the woman's thoughts: 'I used to think she was normal, but now I'm not so sure!'

They hurry off as though they're afraid they'll catch whatever I've got.

Oh well, make a joyful noise...

Quite a crowd has gathered in spite of the rain, but we're really getting into the flow now and no longer worrying about how we look. We really belt out the next few numbers. It's great.

An old man comes up to Simon in the gap before the next song, and shakes his hand. 'You look like you're enjoying yourselves.'

Carol and I look at each other and exchange grins. We are, we really are, because finally we're focusing on who God is and how much we love him rather than on our surroundings. Who cares if we look a bit ridiculous?

✣

Noah's wife must have felt the same pressure of embarrassment, only more so. Her husband was engaged in an unusual building project, to say the least.

It certainly wasn't easy when friends and neighbours stopped by to ask about the structure going up in their back garden. How she wished she could say it was an extension, like the one Abigail was having down the road—something she could boast about, not something she wished she could cover up.

At first it wasn't so bad. It could have been anything in the early stages. But as work continued, it was obvious that this wasn't just an ordinary house-building project. After all, what house was built with a prow?

It seemed that every day more and more people stopped by the building site to watch Noah at work—the neighbourhood hadn't seen anything so exciting for years.

Noah was lucky. He seemed oblivious to the stir he was making. He didn't even notice the stares, and as for the jokes, they just seemed to run off him like water off a duck's back.

'Where's the water, Noah?' Loud roars of laughter.

When she got upset, Noah just kept on saying, 'You'll see. God told me to do it. There's a flood coming.'

And that was before the animals of every size and shape started arriving. The noise was deafening—and the smell...!

'Noah,' she said, on the verge of tears as she tried to shove a stubborn goat into a pen on the second deck, 'you'd better be right about this!'

She and Noah tried to talk to friends and neighbours about what God said was going to happen, urging them to repent, to turn back to God before it was too late.

'Flood, what flood?' they said, looking at the brilliant blue sky with not a cloud in it. 'There's been no flood in living memory. Have you gone crazy?'

Then the rain began. Heavier and heavier. And the water level rose higher and higher until every living thing was swept away, but within the boat Noah had built according to God's instructions, they were all safe and dry.

How thankful she was then for her husband's 'foolishness'—that he had trusted God rather than those who had scoffed and mocked.

It's often hardest to deal with people's reactions, isn't it? Especially as, sometimes, the people who are most judgmental are those closest to us.

When David brought the ark of the covenant—the golden chest containing the Ten Commandments—into Jerusalem, it was a time of great celebration and rejoicing.

We are told in 2 Samuel 6:14 that David 'danced before the Lord with all his might'. He wasn't content with a stately ceremonial walk, or even a few dancing steps. He was 'leaping and dancing' (v. 16), regardless of what those around him thought, expressing his delight in God wholeheartedly and without restraint.

You would have expected Michal, David's wife, to understand his passion to express love for his Lord with every fibre of his body. After all, David had been an outcast for many years, continually on the run from Saul and in fear for his life, and yet now he was the king of all Israel.

Michal was not impressed, however. Why couldn't her husband act as a king should, with reserve and dignity? He was letting it all hang out. And, in her opinion, looking very silly in the process.

Michal could not identify with David's total abandonment to God. In fact, she despised him.

Michal's reaction is a common one. It's all right to love God, providing you don't go 'over the top'. Keep everything within the bounds of good taste. You want to serve God, but don't go overboard about it—if you're too enthusiastic, you're likely to be labelled a religious fanatic.

David's response to Michal's scathing contempt was a simple one: 'I will become even more undignified than this, and I will be humiliated in my own eyes' (v. 22).

David wasn't dancing to impress his wife. He didn't care whether he looked foolish to her, or even to himself. All that mattered was his heart's response to God.

Are you willing to look foolish for God? To openly declare your love for him, even if it earns you a few strange looks?

- Talk about God as enthusiastically as you did about that programme you watched last night on the television.
- Sing to him as you go about your daily tasks, letting him know how much you love him.
- And maybe—who knows?—dance for him as David did! Even if it's just in the privacy of your own bedroom.

Don't worry about how you may appear to others.
Foolish you may be, in people's eyes.
But not in God's.

18 March

All I could think of in church this morning was the argument that Steve and I had in the car on the way.

It had blown up out of nowhere, and quickly got to the stage where we were lobbing insults at each other.

'What about the time when you…?'

'Oh, you always say that…'

'Why can't you…?'

'Why can't *you*…?'

Stalemate.

And of course I know it's all his fault. Because it definitely isn't mine.

My face feels tight as I struggle to worship, and the prayers are just so many words. I can't concentrate.

It's amazing how well we manage to cover up the fact that although we're sitting next to each other, in spirit we're a million miles away.

We're even talking to each other, though very politely and stiffly, and as if we've only just met.

I feel as if there's a big black arrow pointing to us saying 'Dysfunctional Couple', but amazingly nobody else seems to have noticed anything wrong… or perhaps they're just being polite.

We're both feeling awful, but neither of us will back down.

'Just look at the way he's behaved, God,' I fume.

God says nothing, but I know what he wants me to do.

✣

God hates disunity, whether in a marriage or in a church.

Just as, after the honeymoon, we find that being committed to each other and learning to live in relationship is much harder than we'd imagined, so in a church the whole business of getting along together is a potential minefield.

The underlying problem is the same in both cases. We are human and that means we make mistakes—lots of them.

Churches are filled with people who are very different from us. Some will be natural soulmates, but with others we may find that we have little or nothing in common.

Then there are the people who rub us up the wrong way. In any situation, you can almost guarantee that the way you feel and the way they feel will be completely opposite. In fact, if we didn't go to the same church, our paths would never naturally cross.

Brash, bold extroverts; shy, retiring introverts; those who like to dot the 'i's and cross the 't's, and those who go with the flow; peacemakers and groundbreakers—they're all there. It's an exciting mix of volatile elements but, as any chemist would warn you, watch out for explosions!

Unity is something that deeply concerns God, and the church is meant to be a place of refuge in our fragmented society. Yet where you get lots of very different people, there will inevitably be friction.

We can be very clever at disguising, sometimes even from ourselves, what is going on behind the scenes. Yes, on the surface everything is fine, but underneath, is our church more of an Accident and Emergency zone than a recovery ward where healing is taking place?

Are people getting needlessly injured by critical remarks or abrasive comments offered for the recipient's good, 'in love'?

Are there isolation units within our congregations that nobody enters unless they have to, and then only for as brief a visit as possible?

You know God loves Bob, who's been going to get himself sorted out ever since you've known him, and Gladys, who drives people away with her non-stop barrage of moans; and yes, of course you'd love to spend time chatting to them. But not today—there's Helen to invite over for coffee, and Dave and Sue have only just got back from Rwanda—so exciting to hear about God's work, and the way he's touching people's hearts over there.

Is infection steadily spreading through little digs and subtle put-downs? 'Oh well, Joan's children really are a bit wild—they've never been properly disciplined.'

'Karen has a bit of a problem with alcohol, you know, but don't tell anyone else. I'm only telling you so that you can pray about it.' Yet somehow the whole church gets to hear, and the problem that was shared confidentially is now an open secret.

We may not actually do it ourselves. It makes us feel uncomfortable, and secretly we may even feel a slight sense of superiority, because of course we would never talk about someone behind their back like that, would we? 'That's not how *real* Christians behave,' we say self-righteously. And yet we do nothing about it. 'It's really none of my business.'

What happens if we're the one who's been hurt? Sometimes we will try to avoid that person, and in a big church it can be quite easy to keep out of one another's way, mixing with them as little as possible.

If we are troubled by our conscience urging us to try to restore the relationship, we brush it off. 'We're just chalk and cheese. There's no way we're ever going to get on.'

Sometimes, sadly, we simply can't face the person who has caused us so much pain, and leave that church altogether, but the wounds fail to heal properly and leave a wariness of getting close to others for fear of being hurt again.

But what if we try a different tack? Nobody ever said that unity would be easy, but as Psalm 133 reminds us, 'How good and pleasant it is when brothers live together in unity! … It is as if the dew of Hermon were falling on Mount Zion. For there the Lord bestows his blessing' (vv. 1, 3).

Blessing comes not from:

- ignoring underlying problems
- estrangement
- a lack of love

It comes where there is:

- unity
- commitment
- wholeness

God's plan is to have a church where the people are so well integrated that they function like the body in the famous passage in 1 Corinthians 12:12–27.

In a body there are so many parts, all playing very different roles. A nostril has little in common with a fingernail, an elbow looks nothing like a big toe, but together they make up a marvellous living organism.

Paul pokes fun at the idea of different parts of the body trying to exist independently, and we join in the laughter. If we hurt one part of our body, the pain is not isolated, but affects the whole body. You may not notice your ear very much until you get earache. Get a splinter beneath your nail and suddenly that nail takes centre stage—you will think of nothing else.

That's how it should be in the church, because we are meant to function as a whole. 'If one part suffers, every part suffers with it; if one part is honoured, every part rejoices with it' (v. 26).

What sort of place is our church?

Is it a place where people come lonely and leave lonely?

Or is it a place where believers embark on the whole exciting process of learning to be a body, where members actively seek unity, and where every attempt is made to heal wounds before they have a chance to fester?

Let's go for it. There are no perfect churches, but sometimes, with God's help, we come close!

23 March

My 'To do' list today was so long that I knew it would take me all day to get to the bottom of it. And that was before the interruptions started...

First the doorbell—someone wanting a petition signed to oppose the closing of the local post office.

Next, two phone calls. The first is a friend I haven't seen for a while, and it's good to catch up with her, but when I put the phone down I'm amazed to find that nearly half an hour has passed.

I've started to make notes for work when the phone rings for the second time. Rushing downstairs to pick it up before it switches to the answerphone, I'm out of breath.

'Oh, sorry, wrong number,' says the caller.

Back upstairs again.

'Mum,' comes a voice. 'Can I have a cup of tea?' Youngest son has woken up. Of course, he's quite old enough to make his own tea, but he's been working very hard for exams recently, and I want to show him some extra TLC, so down I go to the kitchen to boil a kettle.

'Thanks, Mum.'

Now at last I can get down to some work. Or can I?

The doorbell goes. It's a neighbour, and I'm trying to get to know people in the road, so I pop the kettle on again, and open a packet of biscuits.

All of this would be absolutely lovely, if only I didn't have the nagging sensation of time slipping away.

The gas man calls to read the meter. It takes only a few minutes, but once more my flow of concentration is broken.

The phone rings again. It's my boss. Someone has fallen ill, and would I cover for them? It's very short notice, but it's in my field and shouldn't take too long.

I agree, but my nerves are beginning to feel more than a little frayed. I already had more than enough to do, not to mention that the house could do with a good clean before the weekend.

I sit at the computer and try to clear my head. Several of my son's friends have arrived, and are helping themselves to lunch to the accompaniment of a bass beat. 'Da boom. Da boom. Da boom.' Why is it impossible for teenagers to listen to *quiet* music?

✣

Interruptions are like city buses: they seldom come singly! Sometimes they can be pleasant interludes, but more often interruptions are as much fun as a persistent fly that, however much we swat it, just won't go away and drives us mad with its buzzing.

The *Oxford English Dictionary* defines 'interruption' as 'a breaking in upon', 'a breaking of continuity', an 'obstruction'. To sum it up: inconvenience.

Have you noticed how meal-times are a prime time for interruptions? You've just sat down to a nice hot dinner, fork poised at the ready for that first succulent mouthful, when the phone or the doorbell rings. How do you react?

We may think we have a pressurized existence, but there's no doubt that Jesus' lifestyle was far more so. For Jesus, interruptions were simply a way of life, and everywhere he went he was faced with many demands for his time and attention.

Jesus was a man on a mission, with only three years to accomplish all the work that the Father had given him to do. Yet, although his time on earth was short, he never seemed to react to interruptions with anger or impatience.

The disciples thought they knew what they were doing when they dealt with the 'interruption' of some children who wanted Jesus to lay his hands on them and pray for them (Matthew 19:13). They reacted with annoyance. What a cheek! Their Master had far more important things to do. Wasn't it obvious how busy he was?

Of course it would have been a different matter if it had been a Pharisee or a rabbi or a rich merchant who was interrupting. There'd be some point in spending time with them—they could be very useful in the cause. But children? What a waste of time! Bustling with importance, the disciples shooed the children away.

Jesus' next words stopped them in their tracks. Far from turning the children away, he was actively encouraging them. 'Let the little children come to me, and do not hinder them; for the kingdom of heaven belongs to such as these' (v. 14).

It was clear that to Jesus the children were not an interruption at all, but just another part of what he had been called to do.

Some interruptions are major events grabbing our attention, while others go almost unnoticed.

When Jesus was on his way to the house of Jairus, an important leader in the synagogue whose daughter was dying (Luke 8:40–48), something caught his attention and made him pause. Something so small that anyone else might have missed it altogether—a tentative touch on his garment.

Jesus was busy, on his way to do something important, a genuine matter of life and death. Surely now, if ever, was the time to ignore the interruption, move swiftly past and continue on his way. Yet he stopped.

What were his words to the woman who had reached out to touch his clothing? A natural response might have been, 'Can't you see I'm busy? Go away.'

But to Jesus, she was far more than an interruption. She was a child of God. 'Daughter, your faith has healed you. Go in peace' (v. 48).

Do we take interruptions in our stride, or do they make us feel annoyed and tense? Perhaps we don't actually say the words, 'Go away, I'm busy' out loud, but our body language gives us away. We look bored, and give surreptitious glances at our watch. It's obvious to the other person that we can't wait for them to go so that we can get back to what we were doing previously.

And yet, if Jesus could spare time for people when he had been ministering all day, shouldn't we be able to cope with a few delays?

What will please God more? That you got to all those meetings on time, cleaned the whole house from top to bottom and met all your deadlines, or that you showed something of God's grace and love to people who crossed your path at inconvenient times?

We can view interruptions as obstructions, or we can see them as opportunities to show grace—perhaps pray for the person rather than wishing them a thousand miles away.

In artistic designs, breaks can become an important part of the overall pattern, and make the finished object even more attractive. In a rushing stream, rocks that the current must pass around will make the water flow even faster for the temporary hiatus.

Treat interruptions with grace, and you may find something surprising. What you thought was an annoying gnat may suddenly spread its wings and reveal itself as a beautiful multi-coloured butterfly!

30 March

I balance the pile of freshly washed and ironed clothes clumsily against the wall and try to open the door to the room that belongs to our youngest son, but it won't budge.

Sighing, I put the washing down and use both hands to push the door. Something's stopping it opening properly, but I manage to squeeze through the gap.

Youngest son Pete is a hump in the bed—he hasn't even stirred. I look around in disbelief. It looks as if a whirlwind has passed through the room, leaving behind a litter of papers, magazines and discarded clothes. Crunch, I've just trodden on a CD cover—fortunately empty.

Normally, I try to have a 'hands off' approach to the boys' rooms. The theory is that when it gets bad enough, they will be prompted by the chaos to clear up. It doesn't seem to be working in Pete's case, though. The room doesn't look as if it's been touched for weeks.

Meanwhile, my father is coming to stay tomorrow, and all my intentions of leaving well alone evaporate. I can't quite face the dent to my pride if he saw the state of this room. Something has got to be done.

I tackle the subject when Pete eventually makes a dishevelled appearance at the breakfast table.

'That room needs to be tidied.'

'Why?' grumbles Pete. 'I like it like that.'

'It's a tip.'

'No, it's not,' he says. 'It's a sign of my creativity. All artists are messy.'

'Humph!'

He senses that particular excuse isn't going to work today. He tries a different tactic.

'Aw, Mum. I'm going out. I promised to meet Nick in town this morning.'

'Well, do this first. It won't take long.'

He turns on The Look—the one that says, 'How can you be so heartless and stop me from doing what I want to do? Don't you realize I have a life?!'

I harden my heart.

'Just do it.'

He groans, and stomps up the stairs.

I clear the dishes, aware of thuds and the odd bang coming from his room. It's not long before he's back downstairs with a bin crammed full of crumpled paper balls, chocolate bar wrappers, and browning apple cores.

He dumps two coffee cups beside the sink. I look briefly inside, but recoil at the sight of a green fur of mould in the bottom. Ugh! I give the cups a quick rinse, and put them hurriedly in the dishwasher.

More thumping, and then a long silence.

'Mum!'

'OK, I'm coming.'

'This all right?'

He has done what he's been asked, sort of, but it's obvious that his heart's not in it.

⁂

I think of times when I'm like that—times when, on the inside, I'm just as reluctant. 'Do I *have* to?' And if I do something, I do it half-heartedly, not really bothering too much.

At the moment, if my little niece, Beth, is asked to do something, her usual response is an emphatic 'No!'

'Beth, put your shoes on.'

'No!'

'Shall Mummy help with your shoes?'

'No!'

'Wave goodbye to Auntie Clare.'

'No!'

We may laugh when it's a child, but adults are often guilty of behaving the same way, although with a little more subtlety.

'I don't want you to be involved in that any more.'
'I know, Lord, but I'm not quite ready to give it up yet.'
'I want you to start something in this town for me.'
'Oh, I couldn't possibly do that, Lord. I'm too shy.'
'I want you to befriend your neighbour.'
'But I don't get on with her!'

Jonah heard God speak: 'Go to the great city of Nineveh and preach against it, because its wickedness has come up before me' (Jonah 1:2). Nineveh had an extremely bad reputation, and Jonah was pretty sure that such a message would not be positively received. His response was a definite rejection of God's command: he decided to run away in the opposite direction. Jonah thought that the principle 'Out of sight, out of mind' would be the solution to the problem.

Of course, it wasn't. When little Beth kept saying, 'No', and wouldn't put her shoes on, her father picked her up and took her out to the car anyway. Jonah had much the same experience.

He had refused to go to Nineveh willingly, so God got him there by other means, involving a terrific storm, a cold dip in the ocean, and a stay in the stomach of a huge fish to bring him to his senses.

God then repeated the exact same command, 'Go to the great city of Nineveh and proclaim to it the message I give you' (Jonah 3:2). This time Jonah went, and as a result Nineveh repented and the city was saved from destruction.

When it comes to us, many of us do want to do what God asks, but somehow we get stuck in the realm of good intentions. Obedience begins in the mind but needs to be carried out in action, as even the best intentions are worth nothing if they just remain in our thought life.

Prayer requests are frequent casualties.

'Of course I'll pray for you, Gill,' we beam when a friend tells us she's considering a career change. 'When's the interview?'

A week later Gill comes over and says, smiling, 'I got the job! Thanks for praying.' And we feel a guilty twinge, because actually we'd totally forgotten about it.

In fact, it's often harder to be obedient in small things, perhaps because they can so easily be overlooked. Remembering to organize rotas, ringing people to remind them about a midweek meeting, obeying a prompting from God to invite Mrs Grumpy for coffee—is it really going to matter too much when it just somehow 'slips my mind'?

Perhaps subconsciously we associate obedience with being a child, and when we reach adulthood we behave as though we have outgrown it. We can think and act for ourselves without anyone telling us what to do, thank you very much. It is a sign of our maturity, or so we think...

Yet if you look back at any sequence of important events in the Bible, where does it start? With simple acts of obedience. Obedience is a catalyst for growth, and when we respond in obedience, something significant happens. God moves.

Sometimes the process of obedience challenges us, because what God is asking just doesn't seem to make sense at all.

'Wash yourself seven times in the river Jordan'? What sort of medical benefit could that possibly have? Naaman, the famous military commander, was outraged. He'd been to some of the most highly skilled doctors in the land. Did the prophet Elisha think he was a complete fool? But when Naaman swallowed his pride and obeyed, he was healed of leprosy (2 Kings 5).

Let down your nets for a catch? Simon the professional fisherman struggled with what he knew in his head—they'd been fishing all night, and there were definitely no fish out there—but obeyed from his heart (Luke 5:1–11). That first small step was just the beginning of a road that led to him becoming one of Jesus' foremost disciples.

'Take your long-awaited son—and kill him' was certainly not what Abraham expected God to say. Had God forgotten that this was Isaac, his precious, much-loved son, and the first in the line of Abraham's descendants that God had promised would be as numerous as grains of sand on the seashore? Yet Abraham was prepared to do even this (Genesis 22:1–18). What costly obedience!

Far from being a sign of childishness, obedience is a sign of maturity, and you will find its hallmark in every great man and woman of faith. Indeed, even God's own Son, Jesus, 'learned obedience' (Hebrews 5:8) when he chose to lay his life down for us on the cross, fulfilling God's great rescue plan for humanity.

No wonder obedience is so highly prized by God. 'Has the Lord as great delight in burnt-offerings and sacrifices, as in obedience to the voice of the Lord?' (1 Samuel 15:22, NRSV).

Unfortunately, obedience does not come naturally to us, any more than it does to children, and all too often we resist and dig in our heels.

Move house? But I don't want to, I've always been happy here.

Change my job? But the salary is only half what I'm getting now.

Get up early to join the prayer group? But you know I can't think straight at that time of day!

'Why, Lord, why?' we clamour. 'Why should I do that when I don't want to?'

And God replies, 'Because I ask you to.'

4 April

Megan rushes in like a whirlwind, laden with heavy shopping bags.

'Lovely to see you, darling!' she gushes. 'Sorry I'm late.'

We order coffee and cakes, and settle down to chat, although my half of the conversation is more a case of making appropriate noises whenever Megan pauses for breath.

'You don't say…'

'Did he really?'

'Well…'

'Mmm…'

That's about all I get time for before Megan dashes on to the next topic. In rapid succession we deal with her relationship with her mother-in-law—it's just a question of who kills whom first; her job—overworked and underpaid; her children—driving her mad; and church—can I swap with her on Sunday as she's going away for a spa break?

'Simon said I was looking a little haggard, darling, and he'd treat me…'

'Of course, Megan, and while we're on the subject of church, you know that Ben's off to Tanzania shortly?'

'How exciting. Lucky Ben!'

I continue, 'Well, we're holding a fund-raising evening for him on the 15th.'

Megan gets out her slim black leather diary, and flips through it. 'Oh darling, I'm sorry—we're going out to the theatre that night.'

'Well, could you make a donation perhaps?'

Megan opens her purse and scrabbles through it. I can't help noticing the wad of carefully folded notes, but to my amazement she drops just two 50p pieces into my hand.

'There, will that do? Must fly—got a hair appointment at twelve. You won't believe how much they charge. Daylight robbery! Oh, sweetie, pick up the bill.

My treat next time. Lovely talking to you...' And she's gone in a waft of expensive perfume.

I can't help thinking about Bert, who responded very differently to Ben's need. Bert is single, recently retired from a poorly paid job, and lives in a small flat.

Ben had told me how Bert had thrust an envelope into his hand after evening service. 'I've prayed about it and I felt the Lord told me to give you this.'

Ben opened the plain brown envelope to reveal not only £50, but also a warmly written letter telling Ben that Bert would be praying for him throughout the trip. At the bottom of the note were several encouraging Bible verses that Bert had jotted down, thinking Ben might find them helpful later.

'Do you think he can afford this?' Ben asked me, anxiously.

Looking at Bert's threadbare jumper that had seen better days, I thought probably not.

'It's what he wants to do.'

✢

Giving is one of the thorniest issues in the Christian life. We'll worship, we'll pray, we'll even study our Bibles, but open our pockets—never! We are part of a culture that, in spite of our material wealth, finds giving money harder than pulling eye-teeth.

We lavish endless funds on ourselves and our homes without any problem, but when it comes to giving to God, it's a whole different issue. Why?

Certainly, many of us are struggling financially. The other day at breakfast, our youngest son asked, 'Mum, don't you think you ought to have a better car?'

This wasn't quite such an altruistic thought as it might at first appear, as the subtext reads, 'Your car is the one I drive, and the fact that it has rust patches and a number plate dating back to the ark does nothing for my image.'

'Son,' I retort, '*you* are our second car!' With one son already at university and the other starting later this year, that's where the equivalent of another better motor goes, so our solid, dependable much-put-upon 'rust bucket' stays.

At least it works—most of the time. I wish the same could be said of our 'first' car. It's going through a period when it seems to have taken up permanent residence at the local garage.

And it's at times like this, when there's too much month at the end of the money, that we feel the temptation to cut down on our giving, or maybe skip it altogether. It's a challenge. Giving always is.

There's always a temptation to think of it as 'my' money. 'My money is for me to spend on what I want. It belongs to me, nobody else.' King David points out in 1 Chronicles 29:14 that actually nothing is further from the truth, for it was never ours in the first place: 'Everything comes from you, and we have given you only what comes from your hand.'

Sometimes we give, but with a restraint, almost a meanness, in our giving. 'I'll give exactly what I should because I know I have a duty to do so, but not a penny more.' Perhaps we need to remember 2 Corinthians 9:6: 'Whoever sows sparingly will also reap sparingly, and whoever sows generously will also reap generously.'

For many of us, although we wouldn't publicly admit to it, there's a sense of 'Yes, Lord, I'll do anything—just don't touch my cash!'

Givers come in many shapes and forms:

- Stingy givers: they give as little as they can.
- Dutiful givers: they give because Christians ought to—it says so in the Bible.
- Reluctant givers: they don't really want to.
- Showy givers: they like people to know that they give—and how much.
- Embarrassed givers: they don't like the collection basket to pass by them without putting something in.
- Unthinking givers: they just put a haphazard amount in—praying about how much God might want them to give just never occurs to them.

- Complaining givers: 'if God only knew what this was costing me!' they think.
- Non-givers: they leave it to everybody else—why should they contribute?
- Faithful givers: they give regularly.
- Sacrificial givers: giving that costs.

There is one very unusual type of giver mentioned in the Bible—the 'hilarious' giver (from the Greek *hilaros* in 2 Corinthians 9:7). I haven't been able to spot many of these, but Jesus met one in the temple.

We read the story in Mark 12:41–44. In the NIV translation, the contrast between givers is strongly emphasized.

The temple treasury was a place where it was easy to get yourself noticed, and some of the rich people made sure they took centre stage. In these verses, we don't find the rich giving discreetly so that no one knew how much they were giving. Instead they 'threw in large amounts' (v. 41)—no doubt making a satisfying clatter. By contrast, the two 'very small copper coins, worth only a fraction of a penny' (v. 42) given by the widow would have made hardly any sound at all as they fell.

The officials counting the money probably turned up their noses. 'Who on earth put that in? Look at it—what can you possibly do with a fraction of a penny?' The large amounts, though, would have been carefully noted and put to one side. 'Now that is generous giving!'

What they were missing was the motivation. The large amounts barely made a dent in the wealth of the rich—they had plenty more back at home. For the widow, it was different. She had lost her husband and was poor. Every penny counted. Perhaps she was tempted to use the money for something else—food, or kindling, or clothing—but her love of God was greater.

For many of us, giving is the Cinderella of the church. It doesn't feel 'spiritual', like worship, or praying, or listening to a sermon, and is often viewed as an optional extra.

But the widow knew that giving was an essential part of her worship to God, and so she gave gladly, without holding anything back. Jesus commended her: 'This poor widow has put more into the treasury than all the others. They all gave out of their wealth; but she, out of her poverty, put in everything—all she had to live on' (vv. 43–44).

This was hilarious giving, outrageous giving, celebrated in heaven by an outbreak of rejoicing at what was truly a love gift to God.

The widow may have been poor in earthly terms, but when it came to her heavenly bank account it was a different matter. She knew a simple truth that we often find hard to grasp.

'"Bring the whole tithe into the storehouse, that there may be food in my house. Test me in this," says the Lord Almighty, "and see if I will not throw open the floodgates of heaven and pour out so much blessing that you will not have room enough for it"' (Malachi 3:10).

You can never, ever, outgive God.

9 April

It's a wet, windy night outside, but that hasn't dampened the spirits of our church homegroup, meeting up for a social in the local pub-cum-restaurant.

The evening has been filled with talk and laughter, but now people are beginning to drift homewards. Steve yawns, 'Let's go, shall we?'

I nod. It's getting late, and the following day is our wedding anniversary. As we've had almost no holiday since moving to the city, we're taking a few days off for a much-needed break.

'We'll splash out a bit, eat out a few times, and go up to London for the day,' my husband promises.

'Sounds good to me.'

We are really looking forward to it, and spending time with our friends seems like the perfect way to begin our holiday.

During the evening we've all been circulating around a big table, talking to other people, but my coat and umbrella are still by the chair where I first sat when we came in.

I pick up my coat and look around for my bag. I thought I'd left it hanging on the back of the chair, but there's nothing there.

Perhaps, I think, I didn't bring it with me after all. We rushed out of the house after a late dinner, so I've probably left it at home—yes, that must be it.

'Did I have my bag with me?' I ask my husband.

'I can't remember.'

I can't, either. Oh, the disadvantages of an ageing memory!

We start to walk down the road to the car with a friend, but then I stop.

'I did have it! Remember, I spilled that wine? I got some tissues out of my bag to mop it up.'

'OK, we'll have to go back,' says Steve wearily.

We look around the table again, check the toilets, and ask the staff who waited on our table, but there's no sign of it.

By now, I'm beginning to feel panicky. I ring my friend who was sitting next to me.

'Your bag was there when I left,' Jan says. 'I should have brought it over to you.'

It's looking more and more as if my bag's been stolen.

We walk back to the car feeling tense and anxious. Unfortunately, my purse was in my bag, with all my credit cards. Now we'll have to cancel them, and there's the nagging worry that they may already have been used to withdraw money from our bank account.

I know the fault is really my own, and that I should have looked after my belongings better, but that doesn't stop me feeling a bit cross with God.

'Lord, couldn't you have protected me? I was doing something for you! You know how much we need this break away, and now we'll have almost no money. It's not fair, God.'

✢

We do have a highly developed sense of fairness right from our early years, when the cry, 'It's not fair' is a frequently used phrase in every child's vocabulary.

With my bag, the situation was largely due to my own carelessness, but what about when it's something out of our control?

- A husband walks out on what you thought was a happy, stable marriage.
- You're made redundant from a job where you've served faithfully for many years.
- One of your children develops a life-threatening disease.
- Caring for an elderly parent becomes increasingly difficult so that you face the prospect of committing them to a nursing home.
- Your heart goes out to innocent victims of a war-torn country, or one ravaged by famine or flood.

What on earth is going on? How can these things happen? I thought God was a God of love, but this doesn't look like love.

'Life's not fair,' one of my uncles used to say. 'You'll just have to get used to it.' In one sense he's right, and the reason is very simple. Since Adam and Eve gave in to temptation, we have been living under enemy rule, and captives in occupied territory do not receive fair treatment.

We're so used to this state of things that we forget it wasn't God's original plan, but we only need to read the Bible to find that God is totally opposed to what is unfair. Over and over again it is emphasized that God is a God of righteousness who hates what is wrong. 'For I, the Lord, love justice…' (Isaiah 61:8).

'It's not fair!' could well have been the cry of the angels as God set in motion his plan to rescue a fallen world, a plan that involved total separation from his beloved Son when Jesus paid the penalty for our sins. It wounded God's heart deeply, but it was the only way:

> *He has sent me to bind up the brokenhearted,*
> *to proclaim freedom for the captives*
> *and release from darkness for the prisoners,*
> *to proclaim the year of the Lord's favour*
> *and the day of vengeance of our God.*
> ISAIAH 61:1–2

Picture the scene. A centurion stands watching as a man is about to be put to death for a crime he didn't commit. The trial has been rigged by a bunch of people who don't like him or what he's been doing. He's supposed to be a criminal, but when he looks at those responsible for condemning him, their gazes fall before his.

There's definitely something different about this man. He catches the centurion's eye, and for one long minute they look at each other. The centurion gets the uncomfortable feeling that somehow this man knows all about him in a way that nobody else ever has or ever will—it's a gaze that penetrates right down to the innermost depths of his soul.

Something inside the centurion wants to cry out, to protest against what is happening: 'This is wrong!' But there's nothing he can do. It's his job, and all he can do is watch.

The centurion has heard about this man. He's a carpenter from Nazareth called Jesus, but if all the stories are to be believed, there's something very special about him. Everybody's heard the tales of a cripple healed here, a blind man regaining his sight there, even someone being raised from the dead.

Yes, there's definitely something different about this Jesus, something that transcends the blood trickling down his face where sharp thorns have scratched his skin, and the raised weals on his body from the beating. The centurion has never seen any convicted criminal like him.

Other things have been said about this man too, things even stranger than all these miracles he's supposed to have done. The rumours are everywhere. People are saying that he's the Messiah, or, even more outrageously, that he's the Son of God.

But that couldn't be true, could it, because what would the Son of God be doing in a place like this? God would never allow his Son to be treated like that. It simply wouldn't be right.

They are positioning the man's body on the cross now, the raw flesh wincing as it comes into contact with roughened wood. Then there's the terrible final sound of the nails being hammered in, smashing flesh and bone.

The centurion has seen men go to the cross before—it's not a pretty finish. Some curse, lips twisted with hate; some cower, wretched; but none has ever looked like this Jesus.

It's the man on the cross who's the criminal, so why does the centurion suddenly get the feeling that it's him who's in the wrong? He has coped with curses, and even turned a deaf ear to anguished cries pleading with him to end the torment, but this he cannot bear.

For what he sees in the eyes of the man who hangs there, bruised and battered, each breath a torment, is something far more terrible. Compassion. Forgiveness. And love.

It's a love that transcends the pain and melts the centurion in a way that he has never experienced before. And all doubt is eradicated from his mind. He knows now, knows with absolute certainty: 'Surely this man was the Son of God!' (Mark 15:39).

SUMMER

Arise, my darling,
my beautiful one, and come with me.
See! The winter is past;
the rains are over and gone.
Flowers appear on the earth;
the season of singing has come,
the cooing of doves
is heard in our land.
The fig tree forms its early fruit;
the blossoming vines spread their fragrance.
Arise, come, my darling;
my beautiful one, come with me.
SONG OF SONGS 2:10–13

5 June

'Just let me sleep,' I groan into my pillow. The alarm has just gone off. It's 6.30am, and all I want to do is roll over and huddle beneath the cosy duvet. Why on earth did I say I'd go out with my friend Sally on one of her practice runs for the marathon?

The flesh surely is weak this morning, and, to be honest, the spirit isn't much better. I force myself to get up and quickly get washed, pulling on comfortable clothing, and lacing up trainers that have been stuffed at the back of the wardrobe since I gave up keep-fit classes.

I fortify myself with several cups of tea, and am halfway through a piece of toast when there's a tap at the door.

I open it to find Sally on the doorstep in full running kit, making me wish I'd at least invested in a new pair of jogging trousers rather than these faded ones with splashes of paint from my last decorating project.

'Ready?'

I nod.

'Right, let's go.'

She's off immediately, loping down the road with those swift, effortless strides that make it look so easy.

I follow, trying to get into some sort of rhythm, suddenly conscious of the fact that I'm nowhere near as fit as I thought I was.

I used to be good at running at school, but the years and middle-age spread have taken their toll. We reach a steep incline, and Sally powers straight up it with no problem at all. I stagger along behind as best I can, and long before I reach the top I've slowed to a crawl.

Sally's waiting for me by the park gates at the top, looking ultra-fit, windswept and beautiful, and barely out of breath.

I stumble towards her, clutching my side where I have an agonizing stitch.

My friend looks me over. 'How are you coping?'

I'd like to be able to reply breezily, 'No problem', but I'm struggling to get enough breath to speak at all. My legs are shaky, and I could do with a long sit down, preferably with my feet up on a sofa.

Sally looks concerned. 'I'll tell you what, you walk for a bit and I'll do laps—you join in when you want to.'

Sally is always kind.

I walk along slowly as she passes me again and again and again, giving me a wave and smile of encouragement each time. 'You're doing fine,' she shouts.

I shake my head.

I try to alternate walking and jogging—after all, I've come out to run with Sally—but the walks get longer, and the jogs are just token efforts, soon abandoned.

I'd love to run a marathon like Sally, I really would. I lose myself in a daydream where I'm leading the field, my head thrown back like Eric Liddell in *Chariots of Fire*, legs pumping so fast they're a blur. 'Sleek' and 'gazelle' are words that spring to mind as I head for the winning tape.

'Hi!'

I almost jump out of my skin. Sally's come up quietly behind me. She looks tired, but glowing.

'Twenty laps—I'll try and make it thirty next time.'

Thirty! I huddle deeper into my sweatshirt.

'Isn't it great? I just feel so energized.'

Energized? I can barely walk!

⁘

Actually, there's a very simple reason for the difference between Sally and me. Training. She didn't reach this point without effort, an effort that has involved many hours of building up stamina and pushing through pain barriers to achieve the next level.

If I went straight to the Paris marathon, and started off with no more preparation than I had today, I would not last long before dropping out. I might want sympathy—'Well, at least I tried'—but I doubt that I would get it. People would just wonder why I had bothered running without adequate preparation.

While nobody expects to be able to turn up and run a marathon, we sometimes act as if we can do just that when it comes to the Christian life.

When we first become Christians, the future seems rosy. I suspect that God has a soft spot for learner Christians, as when we start out, every prayer we pray seems to be answered immediately, and we're full of enthusiasm.

The race seems so easy at this point. We can't understand why everybody isn't running—how could anybody not want to do what we're doing? We're full of energy and powering ahead.

However, when we've been Christians for a while, that first burst of speed can slacken off. Our feet hurt, our hearts are pounding, and we're really not sure how we're going to cope with the next stretch. We've been running for a while, and the finishing tape is still nowhere in sight.

If we're not careful, we begin to lose our focus. Instead of looking ahead, we keep looking back over our shoulder at the other runners, and our hearts sink. Other people are catching us up, and some are even overtaking. We're losing our position in the race and falling behind. It's obvious we're never going to be able to catch up again.

We see other runners limp to the sidelines, looking exhausted. Some of them are angry, and we can't help overhearing what they say.

'Nobody said it would be such hard work. I thought we were meant to be getting prizes.'

'I didn't expect the race to be like this. I'd never have joined in the first place if I'd known.'

Other runners have dropped out altogether, and have almost forgotten what the whole experience felt like. Nowadays, they much prefer the role of spectator. They're quite happy to watch from the sidelines and applaud, but don't ask them to be involved.

'Of course I used to run, but I no longer feel the same urge. I've hung up my trainers and retired to the stands. Let other people do the running now.'

Your step falters, and you slow down. Is the race worthwhile after all? Are they right?

Sadly, it's happening all the time—runners leaving the race. Paul challenges the Galatians in Galatians 5:7: 'You were running a good race. Who cut in on you and kept you from obeying the truth?'

Every athlete will tell you that there are points in the race when to give up seems the most natural solution, and when, physically speaking, they've had more than enough. However, they've learned to ignore the nagging voice of discouragement that tells them to walk away from the challenge—that is not the way to win a race.

Running a spiritual race brings its own obstacles to overcome. Don't you think that Moses often felt like giving up as he and the people of Israel wandered in the desert? What was the point of it all? And what about Abraham as he waited year after year for the son God had promised? When would it end?

These were no quick sprints, just a short dash to the finishing line, but long-distance marathons, digging deep into what God had promised and refusing to listen to the voice of negativity. They ran, and kept running.

To run well, we need to keep the goal in sight, the eventual finishing tape. Paul admonishes us to run with purpose: 'Run in such a way as to get the prize… I do not run like a man running aimlessly' (1 Corinthians 9:24, 26).

Nobody is going to win a race if all they are concentrating on is keeping up with everybody else. Actually, you won't be able to anyway, for nobody is running quite the same race as you. We all follow a different course, although ultimately the goal is the same.

And if you fall, don't worry. In the course of life, we will all stumble at times, but that doesn't disqualify us from continuing. We just need to confess our mistakes, learn from them, get up again and continue the race.

The good news is that God's running shoes do not wear out, and many of us, as we grow older in the faith, get our second wind. Our physical bodies may not be in such good shape, but spiritually we are learning to run better daily, experiencing the truth of Isaiah 40:31:

> *But those who hope in the Lord*
> *will renew their strength.*
> *They will soar on wings like eagles;*
> *they will run and not grow weary,*
> *they will walk and not be faint.*

11 June

I bang impatiently on the bathroom door. 'You're not going to be much longer, are you?'

The only reply is an exasperated snort.

It's another ten minutes before the door is finally unlocked, releasing a cloud of steam.

Steve sniffs suspiciously. 'Isn't that my aftershave?'

'Probably.'

We look at each other. Aftershave? What has come over our son? Just a few months ago he would have spent as few minutes as possible in the bathroom. Now it's been… how long?

'At least half an hour,' says Steve, disbelievingly.

A short time afterwards, David comes in, looking slightly sheepish. He's not wearing one of his everyday faded T-shirts, but a shirt and a smart jacket. Even his shoes have been polished.

'Well, what do you think?'

'You look great,' I reassure him.

He relaxes a bit.

'Can I borrow the car, please, Dad?'

'As long as it comes back in one piece.'

'See you later.'

We hear the car drive off.

Oh, the agonies of first love…

❖

Do you remember the first date? The hours spent in front of the mirror, the trying on and discarding of different outfits, searching for that perfect look—perhaps even buying a whole new outfit, because nothing we've got is quite right.

When we go out with someone for the first time, what do we know about the other person? Very little, generally. We may have an idea inside our head of what they will say and how they will behave, but the reality is likely to prove very different.

If we are serious about someone, we will want to see them again, and as the relationship develops, we begin to understand how they tick, what music they like, what their favourite food is, and whether they are a morning or an evening person.

Sadly, for some of us, our relationship with God has never progressed far beyond that first date. We still feel we're in the beginning stages of getting to know him, and we're not sure how much deeper we want to go.

Of course, we dress up in nice clothes to come into his presence, but somehow we don't really want to talk to him, to share our deepest feelings, our hopes and dreams, our fears and frustrations.

After all, he does seem to demand an awful lot. Doesn't he realize that I've got my own life to live? I simply can't spare any more time than I already do. A quick chat once or twice a week is all I can manage right now. After all, that's far better than a lot of my friends —they don't see him at all. At least I know who he is, even if it's just a nodding acquaintance. Isn't that good enough?

Imagine the scene. It's the best restaurant in town. The setting is perfect, candles are on the table, and your beloved is gazing at you adoringly. But you don't even look in his direction.

Or imagine this conversation with your beloved.

'Darling, I really want to spend as much time as possible with you.'

And you say, 'Sorry, I've got to get the shopping.'

Or, 'Sorry, I'm too tired.'

Or, 'My favourite TV programme is on tonight and I can't possibly miss it.'

God will never be satisfied with that. He doesn't want a casual relationship. Ultimately, he wants a bride.

Have you ever been let down by someone you love? Of course you have. It's human nature.

Maybe it's the painful realization that the other person doesn't understand how upset you feel, or the searing pain of rejection that accompanies marital breakdown. Most human love is covered with sticking plasters where cracks have been mended.

But there is a love that is different.

It's a love where nothing is hidden from the beloved, nothing at all. All those embarrassing little character traits, all those mean things you've done that you hoped nobody would ever find out about—he knows.

But what is his response?

Does he turn away and say, 'No, I'm sorry, I just can't love you now I know what you're really like.'

No, far from it—he loves us all the more. In fact, he couldn't be more passionate about us.

Did you know that the Bible contains little love notes?

'I love those who love me…' (Proverbs 8:17).

'I have loved you with an everlasting love…' (Jeremiah 31:3).

'How beautiful you are, my darling! Oh, how beautiful!' (Song of Songs 4:1).

You will never, ever find another love like this.

Are you ready to receive it?

22 June

Every time I go to hang the washing out, I have to battle with an overgrown shrub. Admittedly, it does look pretty when it's smothered in small yellow flowers, but unfortunately there's a darker side to this attractive-looking bush.

The whole plant is infested with greenfly, and they seem to be some kind of super-strain. We've sprayed the little pests several times, but just when we've congratulated ourselves that the problem is solved, they reappear in even greater numbers than before.

Once again this morning, when I accidentally brush against the shrub while hanging up the wet clothing, I'm liberally powdered with translucent green creepy-crawlies—yuk!

The bush also has another drawback. Because it is so tall and spindly, the top branches catch in the mechanism of our antiquated pulley washing-line so that it sticks fast. It happens two or three times a week, and today is one of those occasions.

Balancing a basket of heavy washing while attempting to jerk the line away from wiry branches holding it in a vice-like grip is not the best way to begin the day.

'I'll dig it up when I've got a spare moment,' said Steve—six months ago!

Tug… 'I've had…' tug… 'enough of…' tug… 'this!'

My patience is not just wearing thin, it has worn right through!

I put the washing down, get out a spade and attack the base of the shrub vigorously. The trouble is that large shrubs are like icebergs—there's much more beneath the surface than you realize.

Heaving and straining, hacking my way through the tangled mass of roots, I'm determined not to give up. The bush is definitely leaning now.

Not much more to do, I encourage myself. Just one more section of root still to tackle. You're almost there, girl.

I give a mighty heave of the spade, and the shrub finally topples over. I stagger back.

Crack! An ominous sound.

Not the bush, unfortunately.

My neck. Ouch! I've really cricked it.

I try to turn my head to the left. Awful shooting pain. I leave the bush on the ground where it lies, wishing I'd listened to my husband.

Every jarringly painful movement I make through the rest of that long, long day reminds me of how stupid I've been to tackle the job on my own without waiting for help.

I'm forced to retire to bed early. Steve brings me a hot drink.

'I think God's given me a word for you,' he says, patting my shoulder.

'Oh yes?' I say suspiciously.

'It's in Deuteronomy 9:13. Couldn't be clearer really, could it?'

'I don't know Deuteronomy that well,' I say weakly.

'Do you want me to read it to you?'

'OK.'

Steve opens his Bible, and clears his throat a few times before beginning to read in the best 'preacher' tradition, slowly and with emphasis.

'And the Lord said to me, "I have seen this people, and they are a stiff-necked people indeed!"'

✜

Strength is an admirable quality, but not if it makes us think we can go it alone. Sometimes we learn this the hard way, and the consequences may be far more serious than a painful neck.

In 1 Samuel 13, Saul found himself in a tricky situation. He had summoned the Israelites to gather beneath his standard to fight the Philistines, and was very aware that he must keep morale high.

The wavering people needed the encouragement of a burnt offering to the Lord, but Samuel, who should have been the one to offer it, had not turned up, even though Saul had waited for the seven days they had agreed upon.

As still nothing happened, people began to quietly slip away, frightened by the gathering masses of the enemy army, 'as numerous as the sand on the seashore' (1 Samuel 13:5).

Saul felt that he was losing control of the situation—a frightening prospect. Restless, he decided that he would have to take the necessary action himself, ignoring the little niggle at the back of his mind that told him this was not a good move.

He made the bad choice, and went ahead with the burnt offering—an offering that he had no business making.

Almost immediately, Samuel turned up, and told Saul that his rash action had cost him the kingship. Saul had thought he was doing the strong thing, but all he was doing was the wrong thing.

Moses also took matters into his own hands. Brought up as a prince in an Egyptian household, he saw himself as a fighter against injustice for his Hebrew kinsfolk. This was probably a genuine, God-given compassion and concern. Moses' mistake was that he didn't wait to find out what God had to say about it.

Moses thought he would be a hero among the Hebrew people when he secretly killed a bullying Egyptian overseer, but they just didn't want to know. He was forced to flee, and spent many years in the desert as a shepherd before God took him in hand and finally made Moses the defender of the Hebrew nation that he had intended all along, not the one that Moses had tried to be.

It is encouraging to know that when God wants us to do something, he equips us with everything we need to accomplish the task that he sets before us. You may feel you are unpromising material, but look at the Bible.

- Moses stuttered.
- Gideon was timid.
- Rahab was a prostitute.
- Peter had problems knowing when to shut up.

So it doesn't matter what sort of person we are. We may struggle to say 'Hello' to a neighbour, or we may love to pack our home with people; we may be shy and retiring, or get a buzz from giving a talk in a crowded room. God can, and does, use any one of us.

'I can do all things through Christ who strengthens me' (Philippians 4:13, AV) is a marvellous verse, and not one to be taken lightly.

'I can do all things…' but that means:

- all things that God has planned for me to do
- *not* 'all things I rather think I'd like to do'
- *and not* 'all things that I allow to pile up on me'

We need to ask ourselves, 'Am I doing what God wants me to do, the things I actually should be doing, or am I doing a whole host of other things that I should never have taken on in the first place?'

If we fill our days with things that aren't part of God's plan for us, it's not surprising that we soon feel drained and lacking in energy.

When we find ourselves in this state, God does not condemn us, but offers words to encourage us again. 'Take my yoke upon you and learn from me… For my yoke is easy and my burden is light' (Matthew 11:29–30).

A yoke of oxen ploughing a field copes with the arduous business of turning the heavy clods of soil because it is not just one ox alone performing the task, but two together, sharing the load.

Jesus is beside us as we go about our daily business. We are not alone, and when we struggle, he is there to take the weight from our shoulders. We find our strength not in ourselves, but in him.

> *It is God who arms me with strength*
> *and makes my way perfect.*
> PSALM 18:32

1 July

I'm in the front row and feeling very conspicuous. I don't know this hymn, and at one point I find myself going up when I should have gone down. Embarrassingly, just at that point everyone else decides to sing very quietly, and my wrong note is only too obvious. I feel myself going red.

I'm already quite nervous, as I'm not used to speaking at meetings. Really, rather than sitting in the position of honour beside the chairwoman, I'd much rather be anonymous in the middle with everyone else.

My throat feels tight, and my hands are clammy. 'Stay calm,' I tell myself, but it's not that easy. I look round for Pat, who's come to support me, and she gives me an encouraging smile and a 'thumbs up' sign. I feel a little better, knowing that she's praying for me.

I run over the opening sentence, which I've tried to fix in my mind, hoping that the rest will follow smoothly. I even practised at home, upstairs in the bedroom where nobody could hear me.

My husband had poked his head around the door. 'I thought I heard something. Talking to yourself —that's not good. Is the stress finally getting to you?' he asks in mock sympathy.

I shuffled my bits of paper together, trying to look business-like and efficient. 'No, I'm trying to time my talk. It's meant to last about 30 minutes.'

'Well, that's not too long,' said Steve encouragingly.

But it seems like forever to me.

When the chairwoman introduces me, my legs feel like jelly as I walk to the front. I hold my notes tightly, clear my throat and begin, trying to remember not to speak too fast.

Some people nod encouragingly as I speak, although at the back, I notice, an old dear has nodded off. It doesn't say much for my ability to hold an audience's attention!

It's a lovely feeling when the talk is over, and I almost skip back to my seat. Afterwards, as I drink my coffee and chat, I notice a young woman hovering nearby, but it's not until almost everyone has gone that she comes up to me.

She's going through a very difficult time. 'I just can't seem to feel God any more. I feel so alone. It's as if I'm shut up in a dark room. I just can't see any hope at all. You probably don't know what I mean.' My heart goes out to her. I too have been in that dark place.

✢

Some years ago, when our youngest son was seriously ill, I went through a time so painful that even now I don't like to think about it. Looking after him demanded all my reserves of energy, especially as during the years I was a full-time carer it was rare to get more than a few hours of uninterrupted sleep each night.

At the time, we had not been attending the local church for long and, although we'd previously been very involved in church activities, when I became virtually housebound as I focused on caring for a sick child, we saw almost nobody.

I would love to say that all this strengthened my Christian faith, but at the time it didn't. I was angry, upset and confused. I felt abandoned both by God and by the church, and I had to learn a hard lesson. I had thought I was relying on God, but it turned out that I had been placing my faith in people. Now that these human relationships had let me down, I was in a terrible state. 'If this is what it's like, I'm not sure I want to be a Christian any more,' I said to myself.

It came to the point where I had to make a choice. I had to choose whether I was going to allow my pain and sense of isolation to control my life, or whether I would continue reaching out to God, even though at that moment he felt so far away.

For many of us, there comes a point when we undergo this equivalent of a stripping down, and face the challenge, 'Just what do you really believe in, and how far are you willing to go for those beliefs?'

This was the test that Job faced. Satan was convinced that righteous Job loved God so much only because God had given him so many blessings. 'Take them away, and it will be a different story,' said the enemy, and so Job lost his family, his possessions and his health.

For us, it can be a shock when we realize that we've actually been following a faith with additions. For me, it was Jesus… and friendships in the church, and when I lost those my faith took a battering. For you it may be:

- Jesus and… reputation
- Jesus and… popularity
- Jesus and… health
- Jesus and… your church role

When the additions are stripped away, what is left behind? Is our faith strong or shaky?

For Shadrach, Meschach and Abednego, standing by what they believed would be tested to the limit (Daniel 3:8–30). Either they bowed down in worship before the golden statue of King Nebuchadnezzar or they would be thrown to their deaths in a blazing furnace.

The three Israelites refused to compromise their faith. 'O Nebuchadnezzar, we have no need to present a defence to you in this matter. If our God whom we serve is able to deliver us from the furnace of blazing fire and out of your hand, O king, let him deliver us. But if not, be it known to you, O king, that we will not serve your gods and we will not worship the golden statue that you have set up' (vv. 16–18, NRSV).

Shadrach, Meshach and Abednego were not going to give up on God, even if they died for it. They thought he was worth the ultimate cost.

We are often prepared to trust God when we hope for a positive outcome, but it can be a different story when that seems to be no longer the case.

'But if not…' Do we still have faith in God in worst-case scenarios, when our circumstances are not going to change for the better? How far are we willing to trust God? Only when things go right, or whatever happens?

Sometimes it's almost as if we think nothing bad should ever happen to us, but life's just not like that. Christians are human, and bad things happen to Christians just as they do to anyone else—things that cause us pain and anguish.

'Lord, my son's in the grip of drugs…'

'Lord, this cancer is eating away at my body…'

'Lord, I thought we were happily married, but now my husband has left me.'

Sometimes such stories have happy endings, but sometimes not. Every year, Christians with cancer die. Every year, Christian marriages founder. Every year, children from Christian homes end up broken, breaking their parents' hearts too.

Of course, we wish and fervently pray that it will be different.

'But if not …'

My godmother faced many years of ill-health and increasing pain, but as her physical frame became more and more damaged, something amazing happened, for her spirit became increasingly stronger and more beautiful. In the midst of pain, like Job, she trusted in God, leaning more and more heavily on him as she grew physically weaker.

At her funeral, the vicar spoke movingly of how he always came away strengthened from visiting her, and how, as the walls of her body became thinner with the approach of death, you could see ever more clearly God shining through her.

When Shadrach, Meshach and Abednego were in the fiery furnace, Nebuchadnezzar rubbed his eyes in disbelief. There should have been only three men, but he could see a fourth figure in the flames with 'the appearance of a god' (v. 25, NRSV). The young Israelites were not alone. Jesus was with them in the fiery heat.

As Job faced catastrophic loss in every area of his life, he felt confused, emotionally battered and bone weary, but one thing kept him going even when everything inside him screamed that it was too much, and he could no longer carry on. In all the mess, there was one constant, rock-sure fact, and Job exulted in the midst of the chaos, 'I know that my Redeemer lives' (Job 19:25).

Our Redeemer is still with us, even when we have to face the hard truth that things are not going to change for the better. Even as we join the ranks of the 'But if nots…', there is nothing to fear.

Fear not, for I have redeemed you;
I have summoned you by name; you are mine.
When you pass through the waters,
I will be with you;
and when you pass through the rivers,
they will not sweep over you.
When you walk through the fire,
you will not be burned;
the flames will not set you ablaze.
For I am the Lord, your God,
the Holy One of Israel, your Saviour.
ISAIAH 43:1–3

24 / 25 July

We're up bright and early in the morning, picking up litter from the grass in preparation for our church's Fun Day on the neighbouring estate.

A bright red and yellow bouncy castle goes up in one corner. Carol looks at it longingly. 'Wouldn't mind having a go on that myself!'

I shake my head. 'Some of us just never grow up.'

'Where do you want this?' Gary staggers over with a cardboard box bulging with bottles of fizzy drink.

'The refreshment table's over there.'

Pat rushes up, looking flustered. 'Are you any good at tying knots?'

A group of us get to work on balloons displaying the church logo, which will be handed out to smaller children.

Speaking of children, there are already a few hovering outside the gate, although it's nowhere near time to open. Some of them seem to have an inbuilt radar that can detect anything of interest within a three-mile radius!

'Can I come in yet?'

'Not quite yet—there's still 20 minutes to go.'

A few minutes later, 'Can I now?'

The sun is shining. We couldn't have a better day for it. Families and kids flock in, enjoying the different stalls and games, and we have a constant stream of visitors, particularly as word spreads that it's totally free.

There are a few scuffles.

'It's not fair. He pushed me!'

'Alice, let someone else have a turn now.'

'Tom, I'm not telling you again. It's time to go!'

We dish out a few plasters for scraped knees, and a few tellings off when some of the older boys get too boisterous.

As we clear up afterwards, though, everyone agrees that it's been a success. The visitors have enjoyed themselves, and so have we.

We hope that it will give the church a face in the neighbourhood, and that now when they hear about something we're doing, they'll recognize us as 'the church that organized the Fun Day', rather than 'those funny people down the road'.

The prizes for the Fun Day are being given out at Sunday morning service, and we're pleased to see a small group from the previous day.

'Does it matter where we sit?'

'No, sit where you like.'

Predictably, they settle for the back row and look around, wondering what's going to happen next, slightly nervous. There's much scraping of chair legs, and giggling.

The service begins. We've tried to make it as user-friendly as possible. Some kids fidget, a few leave, but most stay.

'It's OK, your church,' one of the boys says to Gary.

We eat charred burgers and rolls afterwards, washed down with leftover fizz. One of the mothers helps herself to ketchup. 'Are you a proper church, then?'

✣

Her words got me thinking.

When someone walks into our church, the first few minutes are absolutely crucial. This is God's house, different from any other building, but how do we show that?

Some churches actually seem to discourage newcomers. They operate rather on the lines of the St Standoffish Church (Non)-Welcoming Guide, as seen through the eyes of Josephine Bloggs (JB), visiting for the first time.

Rule 1: If you notice a person standing on their own, always give them a wide berth.
JB: Have I got something catching?
Rule 2: Look through the visitor as if they don't exist, but hug the person standing right next to them.

JB:	Will someone talk to me?
Rule 3:	If you do say 'Hello', don't look them in the eye. Walk past as quickly as possible.
JB:	Excuse me, where's the… (voice fading as she realizes nobody's paying any attention) … loo?
Rule 4:	Talk animatedly in a large group. If a visitor hovers on the edge, wanting to join in, break off conversation and move swiftly in different directions, regrouping elsewhere.
JB:	Isn't anyone going to ask my name?
Rule 5:	Don't show visitors to a seat. Wait for them to find their own, then, after a few minutes, ask them to move because that seat's reserved.
JB:	That's the last time I come here!

At other times, the welcome you get when you visit a church for the first time depends on the impression you make. If you look as though you will fit in, wear the right clothes, and speak more or less the same language, then we're only too happy to have you.

But what happens if someone comes to our service who simply doesn't fit comfortably into our church member 'norms'? What if they stumble into a seat, obviously the worse for drink, or dress in a way that, quite frankly, shocks us?

Do these people receive just as warm a welcome, or is it noticeably cooler? Perhaps we excuse our reaction: 'If we have people like that, it will put other people off from joining the church.'

'They'll be a constant drain on our resources. There are organizations where they'll be able to get all the help they need.'

Subtly, we hang out 'This is not the place for you' signs in our words and body language.

Jesus was completely different. Although he met people from every walk of life, from learned theologians to lepers, from worldly-wise tax collectors to rough-and-ready fishermen, his approach never varied. He gave each of them unconditional love and acceptance, and showed them the way to God the Father.

It was the same for us when we first met him, and we were

certainly far from perfect! In Jesus' eyes all human beings are fallible, broken and marred, but infinitely lovable and worth the price of the cross.

Our vision is limited, so we need to ask Jesus to help us to see people as he sees them. Then, instead of wishing that needy people would take themselves and their problems elsewhere, we will be able to react with compassion.

Can you imagine how the leper must have felt when Jesus walked into his life (Luke 5:12–14)? How long had it been since anyone had reacted to him other than with fear, loathing or pity? And yet here was someone who gave him back his dignity, treated him as though he was of worth, and touched him with a loving hand—something that for years he had only been able to dream about.

That is what should make our churches different. The process of growth is messy, as any mother of a baby or toddler will tell you, but there's nothing more exciting than seeing lives changed by the power of God.

People will come to our churches from every sort of background, but every person is equally precious to God. The question is not so much 'Can we show love and acceptance to each one just as Jesus did?' but 'Dare we do anything else?'

29 July

'Is this for you?' asked the postman, handing me a postcard.

I could see why he was puzzled. The postcard was addressed to 'The Duck'.

'Er, yes,' I said, taking it from him hurriedly. The Duck was getting mail?

The Duck had arrived some weeks earlier. One morning the doorbell rang loudly, but by the time I hurried downstairs and opened the door, there was apparently nobody there.

However, the doorstep was not completely empty. On it stood a large wooden duck with black beady eyes, and a label attached to its neck by a pink ribbon: 'Please look after this duck.'

I walked out of the gate and looked up and down the road, but the street was empty. Nobody was in sight. Hmm… very curious.

Steve and I asked everybody we knew about the duck's sudden appearance, but one and all protested their innocence, and in a church with lots of students there were more than the usual number of suspects!

We just couldn't work it out. Someone we knew must have put the duck there, but who? The mystery remained unsolved, and now there was this.

I looked at the postcard—of a duck, of course!—and read:

'Dear Duck.
Just a little Ducky Poem
To say I hope you settle in your new home.
A word of warning on your landlords:
They have a taste for Duck L'orange
Closely followed by blancmange.
Careful what you say, one's a journo,
The other may decide to pickle you in Pernod.
Love, Aunt Jemima.'

Whoever it was, they certainly had a quirky sense of humour.

After dinner, my husband and I settled down with our cups of coffee, and examined the postcard in detail.

'Who can it be from?'

Steve looked for a postmark, but there wasn't one. He turned the postcard over, and looked carefully for clues. 'The card's printed in Hertfordshire. Who lives there?'

'Could it be John? He's up that way.'

'It's the sort of thing he'd do.'

Steve took out his mobile phone. 'Right, I'm going to check it out.' He tapped out a text message. 'What do you think of this?'

I read the message: 'Duckyboo says "Quack!" to Aunt Jemima.'

'Well, it's certainly cryptic. Just one problem—if it's not him, he's going to think you're mad.'

'He won't know it's me.'

A few minutes later we got a text back. 'Who is this?!!'

Oops. Either John was very good at appearing innocent, or he really didn't know anything about our little wooden friend.

I put the postcard by the duck on our kitchen sideboard. 'You know who sent this, don't you?' I accused it.

The duck smirked at me, its black beady eyes glinting. It wasn't giving anything away.

✣

Some friends send cards, some send flowers—and some send wooden ducks! The joy of friendship is that it's so rich and varied. Friends come in all shapes and sizes—some make us laugh, some we share our soul with, some ask questions that make us think, some are similar to us in personality, some couldn't be more different.

In Proverbs 18:24 we read, 'Some friends play at friendship but a true friend sticks closer than one's nearest kin' (NRSV).

If you're on the receiving end of someone who's just playing at friendship, there will come a time when the playing stops. Probably most people know the feeling of having been let down by someone they considered a friend—it is somehow much harder to deal with than if a colleague, or someone we don't particularly get on with anyway, did the same thing, and it causes us much pain.

Friendship is all about consistency. We need to be there for our friends when they go through hard times, to provide a sounding board when they need to talk things out, or a shoulder to cry on in times of stress. When my mother died, one of the things I most appreciated was the support of my friends. 'Just pick up the phone if you need me, and I'll be right there,' said one note.

Good friendships bring out all that is best in us. 'As iron sharpens iron, so one person sharpens another' (Proverbs 27:17). A good friend can spur us on to do things that we would perhaps never dare to do without their encouragement.

Jonathan's constant support, encouragement, and vision for his friend helped David to take on the kingship of Israel. We should never be afraid to dream big dreams for our friends.

Although there is no room for jealousy in friendship, friends sometimes use tough love. 'Faithful are the wounds of a friend,' says Proverbs 27:6 (AV).

It takes a brave and wise friend to challenge us when we're beginning to wander off track, to point out that we've lost sight of our original vision, or to caution us when we're walking towards something harmful—perhaps the temptation of an extramarital affair, or mixing with people who steadily undermine our faith rather than helping us grow in Christ.

Unfortunately, we live in a world where the normal pace of life is hectic, and it is easy to lose sight of our friendships. A dear friend moves away, and at first we phone and write regularly, but then as other matters fill our lives, the contact is loosened until perhaps we only exchange Christmas letters.

'To lose a friend is to die a little,' goes the saying, and Proverbs 27:10 also cautions, 'Do not forsake your friend.' Friends should be cherished and nurtured, for they enrich our lives so much.

Jesus values friendship extremely highly. 'Greater love has no one than this, to lay down one's life for one's friends. You are my friends if you do what I command' (John 15:13–14).

It doesn't seem possible that the Son of God should want to be our friend, but that is the truth. Jesus could so easily have treated us as servants, but he doesn't want people who will just obey his orders out of a sense of duty. He wants more than that.

Maybe we feel we're not good enough to be Jesus' friend, but he was known as 'a friend of tax collectors and "sinners"' (Luke 7:34). He loves us, warts and all, and his heart is big enough to accept anybody who invites him into their lives.

As we learn to walk in friendship with our God as Moses and Abraham did (Exodus 33:11; 2 Chronicles 20:7), we discover a friendship that is rock-like, that will never fail us or let us down.

In the Song of Songs, the woman speaks of her lover in terms of great passion—she cannot wait to see him and embrace him. He is not only her lover, but also her closest friend.

Can we identify with her joyous introduction of her lord? 'This is my lover, this my friend, O daughters of Jerusalem' (Song of Songs 5:16).

1 August

We were up with the lark this morning to pack the car for our annual camping holiday up in the Midlands, a journey of three to four hours if you get an early start. We hoped to arrive soon after lunch, get the tent up, unpack everything, and then have a few hours' rest before the evening's activities.

We were making really good progress, and looking forward to a welcome coffee break, when Steve suddenly exclaimed, 'I've left the inner tent behind!'

I laughed. He wasn't going to fool me. Last year we'd realized after we'd driven about forty miles that we'd left the camping stove at home, and had to turn back for it.

Now he thought it would be funny if he pretended he'd done the same thing again. As if we could have forgotten the inner tent! It was so large, and an integral part of the tent itself. I knew my husband's sense of humour of old.

I calmly helped myself to a peppermint. 'Oh dear.'

Steve began to slow down.

'What are you doing?'

'I told you. The inner tent's not in. We're going to have to turn back.'

I looked at him. 'You *are* joking, right?'

'No, I'm not. I wish I was.'

'But we're over halfway…'

'I know.'

'Can't we just go on without it?'

'Not really, it'll get too cold at night. We'll have to turn back. Sorry.'

I could feel steam building up between my ears, but clenched my teeth, telling myself to keep calm. On a long journey, arguing would simply make matters worse.

✣

It would have been so tempting just to carry on and try to cope without this vital part of our equipment, but if we'd done that, our camping holiday would actually not have been so good. It was a painful decision to make, but in the end it was the best one in the circumstances.

Turning back is one of the hardest choices to make, particularly when we have come a long way from the point to which we will have to return. Something inside us says that to do such a thing is an admission of failure. Surely it can never be good to have to go right back to the beginning?

'You don't want to do that. How pointless to leave where you are and go back—you've already been that way once. What good will it do to go that way again? You'd only be wasting your time. Just keep going, and forget all about it.'

Sometimes, though, retracing our steps is exactly what God wants us to do. If you're knitting and drop a stitch or two, you can leave the loose loops of wool, but they will not only spoil the overall appearance of what you are making, but will also be a point of weakness.

It's frustrating, but the only way to get the finished article looking as it should is to go back to where the stitches were dropped, and pick them up before continuing. It's just the same in sewing. If you have a seam where the stitching has gone awry, the only solution is to unpick the crooked part and start again.

Dropped stitches—perhaps somewhere along the path of our Christian life we have left things behind that we actually need for the journey ahead, that we need to retrieve before we can continue on our way.

Are you feeling disillusioned and battered by some rough experiences? Ask God to heal you and restore the enthusiasm you used to have.

Are you cynical? 'I've seen it all before. It didn't work then, and it won't work now.' Ask God to rekindle your faith.

Do you feel spiritually dry and unable to reach out to others? Ask God to give you his love for those around you.

Sometimes it seems that it's not just a few stitches but the actual stitcher that desperately needs recovery.

The prodigal son got into a real mess (Luke 15:11–32). He left his father's values far behind, and went as far away from his previous lifestyle as he possibly could. He thought he could find happiness by living a hedonistic life of pleasure, not caring about possible consequences.

Soon the inheritance that his father had generously given him was used up, and so was he, left high and dry by his new 'friends', and so hungry that he even ate food set aside for the pigs he was tending. The glittering lifestyle that had dazzled him turned out to be hollow and empty.

Coming to his senses was painful. It's not easy to admit that you've gone wrong, and that the way you've chosen to travel has in fact been a dead end.

The son had just two choices. To continue as he was, having once known life with the father, but still pursuing a road away from him; or to retrace his steps all the way back to where he had started, to his father's house.

He chose to return to his father, thinking that things could never be the same between them again. He had been a much-loved son, but, after all that had happened, surely he had destroyed the relationship between them for ever.

From now on, he could only hope to take the place of a servant in his father's household. He had recklessly thrown away any claim to his father's love by his selfish, destructive behaviour.

The son's steps slowed as he got nearer and nearer to the family home. He remembered that wall—he and his brother had often sat on it side by side, watching the herds of goats pass by. In those days he had still been the apple of his father's eye. His life was not then marred and spoilt. Shame made him hang his head.

From a distance someone saw him coming, someone who had never ceased to love and long for his wayward son, someone who now ran as fast as he could to take the ragged dirty boy in his arms, weep, and hug him. The father's boy was home, home to enjoy the father's love once again.

It doesn't matter how far we've gone down the road—there is always the option of returning home.

If you've been away, perhaps abroad, for a long time, and are finally returning to a well-loved place, you will know the excitement of seeing familiar signposts that tell you you're getting close to your destination.

How our heart quickens as we come around the final bend and there it is—home, the place we love so well, the place where we belong.

For those who believe in God, there can be no better place to come home than to him, to his all-embracing love. It doesn't matter how long you've been away, it doesn't matter what you've done—he just longs for you to return.

'"Return to me, and I will return to you," says the Lord Almighty' (Malachi 3:7).

It's time to turn back, time to come home.

Why wait any longer?

3 August

High summer, and the Bible Week is in full swing. Oh, the joys of sleeping under canvas on a lumpy airbed, and eating meals out of packets and tins.

Every morning I stand, washbag in hand, in the long queue for what seems like hours, waiting for a shower. 'What's it like?' I ask Pat, ever hopeful, because there have been times when the temperature has been vaguely warm.

'Freezing!' It's the answer I really didn't want to hear. Long leisurely showers, basking in the warmth of the water, are a far-distant memory. This is more like a test of endurance as I brace myself to step beneath the bone-numbing spray. I get washed at a speed that could win an Olympic medal.

After that, it's a quick trip to the mobile loo—another Bible Week treat, with its bouncy floor—a small cramped space where you definitely would not be able to swing a cat (and who would want to swing a cat anyway?!)

The worst time is late at night when I'm snugly tucked up in my sleeping bag. I toss and turn, willing myself to go to sleep, but it's no good.

'Remind me why we do this?' I complain as I wedge my feet into wellies for my second late-night trek to the loo block.

Who would guess that in such conditions, in draughty animal halls still smelling strongly of cows despite the carpets laid down, you could experience a foretaste of heaven?

✣

A taste of heaven is found in the oddest places. For Jacob it involved bare earth and boulders—an unpromising landscape, but one where God touched him and changed his life forever.

As a young man, Jacob was probably not a very pleasant person. He was clever and he knew it, never missing an opportunity to outwit his elder brother.

The two brothers could not have been more different. Esau enjoyed hunting and was definitely a macho type, while Jacob was his mother's favourite and stayed at home.

However, while Jacob lacked muscle power, he could run rings round his brother when it came to mental agility.

When Esau returned hungry from working in the fields one day, Jacob was cooking a tasty stew. How good it smelled, and how Esau's empty stomach longed for a helping (Genesis 25:29–30).

Jacob immediately spotted an opportunity and grabbed it with both hands. 'Of course you can have some stew. But only if you sell me your birthright.' Wily Jacob! He knew Esau's appetite would get the better of him (vv. 31–34).

And Jacob didn't stop at Esau's birthright—the privileges that came with being the elder son. He quickly consented to his mother's audacious scheme to con his big brother out of Isaac's blessing too (Genesis 27:1–40). The fact that it also involved deceiving his elderly father seemed to make him hesitate only momentarily. Jacob's name meant 'supplanter', and how well it suited him!

All went according to plan, except that Jacob seriously underestimated the force of his brother's reaction. Esau was absolutely furious, and Jacob quickly discovered that his brother was not going to let him get away with it this time. Frightened, Jacob had no choice but to flee from his brother's wrath.

It must have been a rude awakening for him. Jacob was used to being protected from his actions, but this time he had gone too far. He could no longer enlist the aid of a kindly father and a doting mother.

Now Jacob was on his own. He didn't even have a comfortable bed to sleep on—just bare earth and a hard stone for his pillow (Genesis 28:11).

Perhaps for the first time in his life, Jacob felt a sense of shame at his behaviour. He had tried to buy God's favour and scheme himself into God's blessing, but even Jacob had to admit that all his efforts had come to nothing.

Where had all his cunning got him? Who was Jacob in the wilderness? Nobody.

He had thought he was on a highway to success, but now it seemed he had come to a dead end. Jacob lay down with his hopes in tatters.

And finally, with Jacob at the lowest point in his fortunes, God was able to speak to him.

Jacob met with God through an amazing dream. Up till now all his dreams had been daydreams about how Jacob could achieve his own selfish ends. This one was different.

He saw a ladder stretching from heaven to earth with angels ascending and descending, and Jacob realized that he was not alone after all. God was in this place.

'I am with you and will watch over you wherever you go, and I will bring you back to this land. I will not leave you until I have done what I have promised you' (Genesis 28:15).

Jacob was not expecting to meet God. He had thought he was in the place of failure, but how wrong he was. He was in the place where God could touch him and speak into his life.

When Jacob awoke, his whole perception of the place had changed because God had visited him there. 'Surely the Lord is in this place, and I was not aware of it' (v. 16).

To others it would have looked like the same old wilderness, but to Jacob it was the 'gate of heaven' (v. 17). Even the lumpy boulder that he had used for a pillow took on a new significance. Jacob raised it up as an altar, a witness to the fact that this was a holy place.

The gate of heaven for Jacob came at a point when he had reached rock bottom, but God turned the whole situation around. Jacob made a new beginning. The difference was that he was no longer in charge—God was.

The amazing thing is that God is willing to meet with us anywhere—it doesn't need to be a wilderness like Jacob's, or even a

Bible Week. There is only one simple requirement—that we put our lives into his loving, capable hands.

We can taste heaven in a hospital bed or in the company of a little child. Heaven can be in our workplace or our kitchen. It can be the front seat of our car, a busy supermarket aisle, or a Damascus Road, but one thing is certain. It will change our lives for ever.

AUTUMN

Where can I go from your Spirit?
Where can I flee from your presence?
If I go up to the heavens, you are there;
if I make my bed in the depths, you are there.
If I rise on the wings of the dawn,
if I settle on the far side of the sea,
even there your hand will guide me,
your right hand will hold me fast.

PSALM 139:7–10

1 September

'You know,' my youngest son says, helping himself to a generous dollop of jam and carefully spreading it on to the thick-cut slice of crusty bread, 'I'm sure that wall's lower than before.'

I come over to the kitchen window and look into the back garden, where two young workmen are busily rebuilding the wall between us and the neighbouring house.

The wall had been so unstable that when you pushed it with your hand it rocked gently to and fro, and it had been a matter of urgency to get it rebuilt.

'Maybe it does,' I concede cautiously. The trouble is that I can't really remember exactly how high it was in the first place.

If only I'd been here earlier, but now the workmen have very nearly finished. They're carefully placing the final row of coping bricks—a tricky task, as the wall slopes at a steep angle. I know I won't be at all popular if I say it needs redoing.

'Mum, you can't leave it like that—it's far too low. Look, you can easily step over it at the top!'

I'm still reluctant. I hate to cause a fuss.

Then I remember that when the house was first surveyed some photos had been taken of problem areas needing attention. Maybe there was a photo of the wall as it used to be.

I leaf through the folder, and there is the wall. Pete is right—it had another nine rows of bricks that made it significantly higher.

Armed with the photographic evidence, I feel slightly braver, but it's still not easy to go out there and do something about it.

'Almost finished,' says Joe, looking at me with a broad grin.

'Erm…' My mouth is dry. 'I'm really sorry, but I'm afraid that wall's not high enough.'

'Not high enough...'

He doesn't actually swear, but you can tell he'd like to.

I show him the photos.

'Look, this is how it was before.'

'Doesn't look that different to me.'

'Well, count the bricks.'

He does, twice, as if hoping the tally will change.

'Nine bricks different—not that much, really.'

He looks up hopefully. 'We could put a nice piece of trellis on top.'

'I'm sorry, but we really do want bricks.'

'Well, you're the boss.'

Fortunately, the cement hasn't had time to set, and the dismantling of the wall doesn't take as long as I feared. The extra nine rows are soon added, if not with a very good grace.

'Nice wall.' Steve pats it in passing. 'Must have been fairly straightforward —more or less a straight run of bricks.'

'What do you think of our wall, Grace?' he calls to our neighbour, who has just come out of her kitchen.

She looks at it carefully. 'Shame about the white bricks.'

'The white bricks?'

Now I look more closely, I realize that instead of putting all the bricks from the white painted section of the original wall together as they were before, the builders have randomly scattered them among the red bricks.

Grace sniffs disapprovingly. 'It looks like one of those—what do you call them?—public conveniences.'

It does, rather.

'But still, never mind—I expect I'll get used to it in time. Probably too late to change it now...'

'Oh yes,' I say hastily, 'I'm afraid so. Much too late.'

❖

Walls are perhaps not the most decorative of features, but they serve an important purpose. Walls mark a boundary, provide protection and shelter, and sometimes act as a means of defence. Without walls, people are free to wander wherever they want and do whatever they like—there is nothing to stop them.

Sometimes walls have an even deeper significance. For Nehemiah, the broken-down walls of Jerusalem were symbolic of the ruinous spiritual state of God's people, and their attitude towards the Lord (Nehemiah 1:6–7). How could Jerusalem have been allowed to fall into this terrible state?

Although Nehemiah was to become perhaps the most important wall builder of all time, he was not the obvious choice for the job. Nehemiah had little experience of hard manual work, for he worked in the luxurious surroundings of a palace, as cupbearer to the great Babylonian king Artaxerxes.

Nehemiah, however, was someone who cared far less about the perks of his job than that God should be honoured. When he heard that the walls of Jerusalem, the holy city of God, were in a state of ruin, heaps of tumbled stones instead of a majestic commanding presence, it caused him deep grief.

Was Nehemiah the only one who noticed what had happened? Of course not. Probably others had walked past the broken-down city walls many times, but they had quickly become used to the sight.

Perhaps they even managed to convince themselves that what had happened was all just part of the natural course of things. 'Things change, that's simply a fact of life, so why waste time trying to turn the clock back? City walls are not for today—they're outmoded, outdated. We've moved on, and there's no real need for them any more.'

But Nehemiah couldn't forget about it. To him, it mattered deeply. He grieved for the walls of God's city, walls that should have been strong and powerful, a witness in the surrounding land, not a broken-down heap of rubble.

As Nehemiah prayed about the situation, he realized that God had laid it on his heart for a reason. How easy, and how tempting, it would have been to leave it to someone else, somebody who already knew how to build walls. He was only a cupbearer—his building skills were minimal—but Nehemiah knew that God wanted him to do something about it.

We read the story of how Nehemiah went about this important building project in the book named after him in the Old Testament. Rebuilding the walls was not an easy task, but one that required commitment and perseverance, and took a long time to complete.

Nehemiah and those helping him faced much discouragement. 'Can they bring the stones back to life from those heaps of rubble—burned as they are?' scoffed Sanballat the Horonite (Nehemiah 4:2).

Some of the people probably looked at the heaps of fallen masonry and wondered if Sanballat was right. It was hard to imagine such a huge task ever reaching completion.

But Nehemiah was not a quitter. He cajoled, he encouraged, and above all he prayed, and stone by stone the walls began to rise. Even then, their enemies continued to persecute them, seeking to make the people lose heart and abandon the task.

'What they are building—if even a fox climbed up on it, he would break down their wall of stones!' (v. 3).

The situation can be the same for us.

'What makes you think Christians can change anything? All your efforts will come to nothing!'

How firm do the walls stand that declare the presence of God in our land, and what sort of condition are they in? Do they stand tall and proud, or have they been broken down in places?

Something happens that contradicts God's laws—something that chips away at what we stand for as Christians—and yet often we're reluctant to do anything about it. We don't want to say that it's wrong. We don't want to make a fuss, and so we excuse ourselves.

'Well, this isn't particularly important. We'll make a stand when it's something that really matters.' And slowly, massive stones that once looked immovable begin to shift from their foundations, bringing closer and closer the day when they will fall, leaving gaping holes behind.

Rather than just turning a blind eye, we need to be vigilant. Are we making sure that the wall is strengthened where it needs to be, and moving to replace stones if there are gaps in the defences, letting things in that should really stay outside?

Nehemiah would not allow fear and intimidation to stop him from rebuilding the wall of Jerusalem until it once more became a thing of glory, a clear boundary defined by God's presence and God's laws.

Perhaps we've put off doing anything because we feel that the task is simply too enormous, but if nobody builds, the wall remains broken down.

Nehemiah's helpers included people from all walks of life, including the high priest and his fellow priests, rulers of districts, the daughters of one of the rulers, perfumers, goldsmiths and merchants.

How many of those people knew how to use a builder's trowel? But they wanted to see the wall restored to its former glory, and as they each worked on individual sections, perhaps just a few feet in some cases, the gaps in the wall steadily closed.

What is God speaking to you about? What does he want you to get involved in?

'But now, O God, strengthen my hands' (Nehemiah 6:9, NRSV) was Nehemiah's constant prayer.

Where are the wall builders of today?

14 September

I'm just having my coffee break when the phone rings. It's Julie, an old friend from the town where we used to live.

'Hi, I was just wondering when the two of you could come over for a meal? It's been a while since we last got together, and it would be great to catch up with how you're getting on.'

'That would be so nice. Hang on, I'll get the calendar.'

'OK, what about the 16th?'

'Steve's away at a conference. We can do the 18th or 19th.'

'We've got visitors then. 26th?'

'That's homegroup. 31st?'

'That's our homegroup.'

It's hard to believe, but the first date we can manage is three months away. We pencil it in.

'Meanwhile, how about if just you and I get together for coffee?'

'OK.'

'12th?

'No, I've got a workshop… 15th?

'There's something on at Jamie's primary school.'

Most of the spaces on our calendar have ink or pencil scribbles. Just yesterday I looked at the week ahead, and saw that 'Pudding Evening' was marked in one of the squares. But where, and what was it connected with? I hadn't a clue.

I rang Jackie to see if she knew anything about it, but she didn't. 'Next time,' she said patiently, 'put a bit more detail.' So somewhere, at an unspecified time, a Pudding Evening will be going on, but I won't be there, unfortunately. Unless it's at our house…!

❖

Do you sometimes feel as if there is so much going on that you don't know whether you are coming or going? Certainly, time in our house is always in short supply. I could do with twice the hours in the day, and even then…!

I've become quite an expert at multi-tasking, and my constant theme song is 'Busy, busy, busy'. Yet I don't really want it to be like that. As I rush from one thing to another, my heart feels a little sore because, more than anything else, I don't want to be the sort of person who doesn't have much time to spare with friends, family or even God.

'Mummy, play with me.'

'Sorry, darling. Mummy's just got to do this. Perhaps later.' But of course, 'later' rarely comes.

'Let's spend some quality time together.'

'I'm sorry, I'm really overtired, and besides, I need to get down to the ironing—otherwise there'll be no clothes ready for tomorrow.'

God waits for me to spend time in his presence to get refreshed and recharged for the day ahead, but it seems that, time and time again, I can only spare a few minutes as I didn't get up early enough yet again.

I wonder why we fill our lives so relentlessly. Just what are we trying to prove?

Periods of rest are actually extremely important, but the trouble with many women is that they feel guilty when they do 'nothing'. There's so much they could be doing—the cooker needs cleaning, bulbs need planting, friends need to be phoned, family fed, washing machine loaded.

It's a shame that with God's awesome creation all around us, so many of us are scarcely aware of it. We need to remind ourselves of Psalm 8:3: 'When I consider your heavens, the work of your fingers…'

Have we been doing much 'considering' recently, or are we always in too much of a rush? We have a lot to learn from children in this respect—the way they just stop what they are doing and take minutes at a time to look really, really hard at something that interests them. Everywhere we go there are marvellous things to discover—maybe a spider's web beaded with dew, richly tinted autumn leaves, or a shiny blue-black beetle scurrying across the pavement.

Take time to stop and to wonder. It will fill your heart with an overwhelming sense of God's blessing as you see the attention he has lavished on the smallest details. The Bible tells us that his creation is one of the ways in which we can most clearly see God's hand—that through it he reveals himself.

Rest is something that God himself enjoys. For six days he worked on his mighty creation, forming the earth, but on the seventh he rested: 'And God blessed the seventh day and made it holy, because on it he rested from all the work of creating that he had done' (Genesis 2:3).

Jesus sent his twelve disciples out to put what he had taught them into practice, to preach the gospel and to heal, and when they returned they were full of what had happened. It had been a time of much fruit, a positive and exciting experience, but did Jesus immediately start to prepare them for the next mission?

No. Instead, he said to them, 'Come with me by yourselves away to a quiet place and get some rest' (Mark 6:31).

Jesus himself also frequently spent time in restfulness, times of quiet in contrast to the business of hectic days when crowds followed to hear his teaching and to be healed. Jesus saw periods of rest as essential to his ministry.

'He went up on a mountainside by himself to pray' (Matthew 14:23).

'One of those days Jesus went out to a mountainside to pray, and spent the night praying to God' (Luke 6:12).

Many of us are not very good at resting. No sooner have we sat down than we begin to feel guilty. 'Shouldn't I be doing the washing-up, hoovering, preparing Bible study notes, marking schoolwork…?'

Just as farmers and gardeners know that soil benefits from a break between crops to achieve the greatest fruitfulness, so we need 'time out' to recharge our batteries.

If we don't, we are not acting wisely, as the more tired we get, the less likely we are to cope under pressure. It's like an elastic band that is continually stretched too tightly. If it is always kept taut, it will lose its elasticity and become saggy (know that feeling?) or it may even break altogether.

After his struggle with the priests of Baal, Elijah was absolutely exhausted, emotionally, physically and spiritually. He had been giving out too much for too long, and it was not surprising that a wave of depression hit him. He felt totally isolated. 'I have had enough, Lord… I am the only one left' (1 Kings 19:4, 10).

What was the solution? Simply rest—sleep, bread baked on hot stones, a jar of water, and time spent with God. Time out.

'Rest in the Lord, and wait patiently for him' (Psalm 37:7, AV).

19 September

You can hear it even from outside the church building—the whine of electric guitars and a pounding drumbeat, and, as you push open the inner door, your ears are assailed by a wave of sound breaking over you.

One of our senior members clutches my arm. Her lips are moving, but I can't hear a thing. I lean my face close to hers to catch what she is saying.

'Will it be quieter when the service starts, do you think?'

I smile at her reassuringly. 'Probably...'

But I have my doubts.

The hall fills up, and the worship leader stands up in front of the microphone. 'Let's all push our chairs back, and get ready to praise the Lord!'

And the band begins with a crash of drums. There's no doubt that the members of the youth group are putting their whole heart and soul into it, but what about the rest of us?

I look nervously at my elderly neighbour. She seems happy enough, nodding her head and smiling, but when she carries on for a few moments after the song has stopped, I realize that her hearing aid is lying in her lap. When the microphone gives a screech like a strangled cat, I wish I was in her shoes.

Some people are really enjoying it, but others are obviously struggling. It's just not their sort of music. Can God really like this stuff?!

Some of the young folk pray enthusiastically, and then it's the last song, which finishes with an extended drum solo. The teenagers clap and cheer. We oldies clap too, our ears still ringing from the volume.

'Well, what did you think?'

'It was certainly different...'

'The songs were OK. It was the volume.'

'Loud.'

'Very loud.'

'Deafening.'

Vera points to the drums. 'It wouldn't be so bad if we didn't have those. It wouldn't be so bad if they were played quietly.'

'And that conga thing—it was more like a party!'

Pat speaks softly. 'Don't you think it's great that we have teenagers who want to praise God? They could be out doing all sorts of other stuff, but they're here…'

✥

What is it that makes us so quick to notice what is wrong in a situation, rather than what is right? It seems all too easy to indulge in a little bit of 'helpful' criticism.

We listen to the speaker, and take great pleasure in pointing out where the poor man (or woman) could improve.

'Oh, I didn't agree with what they said about…'

For us, the sermon is too long… too dull… not practical enough… not spiritual enough.

And then we tackle the worship.

'Oh, I couldn't really get into it…'

'It was too noisy.'

'The Spirit wasn't really moving.'

It's equally easy to see others' faults. It's funny how the fact that Mary has a quick temper is glaringly obvious to us, and yet we fail to recognize that we too have a short fuse. But then, of course, for us it's 'understandable'.

We put it down to PMT, or the menopause, or the children driving us mad, or the fact that we've had a long, tiring week. We excuse ourselves, but Mary—that's a different matter.

Jesus challenges us, 'Why do you look at the speck of sawdust in someone else's eye and pay no attention to the plank in your own eye? How can you say, "Friend, let me take the speck out of your eye," when you yourself fail to see the plank in your own eye? You hypocrite, first take the plank out of your eye, and then you will see clearly to remove the speck from the other person's eye' (Luke 6:41–42).

There is a flip side to the pervasive cancer of criticism—something that stops it in its tracks, and causes it to wither and die. A praising heart is one of the most godly qualities that a Christian can possess, and one that God himself cherishes.

We know that praise is important as it is mentioned over and over again in the Bible. God's people are meant to be a praising people. It is not an optional extra, although you might think so when meeting up with some churchgoers!

Psalm 34:1 says, 'I will bless the Lord at all times; his praise shall continually be in my mouth' (NRSV).

It sounds so simple, but there's no doubt that an attitude of praise is not always easy even when everything's going well, let alone when we're ill or hurt, or when nothing seems to be going right.

'I just don't feel like praising God this morning,' we say glumly, but praise is not meant to be just a feel-good option. Praising God when everything within us screams against it—a true 'sacrifice' of praise—is very precious in God's sight.

For Paul and Silas, humanly speaking, it had not been a good day. First they got on the wrong side of the owners of a slave girl, who were furious when Paul and Silas commanded a spirit of divination to leave her in Jesus' name (Acts 16:16–18).

Her fortune-telling talents had made her masters a good deal of money, and, with their income gone, they wanted revenge. They dragged Paul and Silas before the authorities, who did nothing as the two men were savagely attacked by the hostile crowd.

In addition, Paul and Silas' clothes were stripped from them, and they were severely beaten with rods before being thrown into prison. Cause for praising God? You wouldn't think so.

That night, however, the prison walls resounded to an unfamiliar sound. Not cursing, or weeping, or even drunken singing, but Paul and Silas praising God in the midst of a painful and difficult situation.

For most of us, this would not be our reaction, because we have not yet become fluent in the language of praise, and yet it is the language of heaven.

So where do we start? Just as with learning a foreign language, we start with the basics, the simplest phrases, until they become so much a part of our vocabulary that we use them without even thinking.

'Thank you.'

'I appreciate you.'

'I love the way you…'

Praise phrases—simple but powerful words that free us from the trap of negativity. Use them when speaking to others daily—and to your heavenly Father who loves to hear them.

> *Because your love is better than life,*
> *my lips will glorify you.*
> *I will praise you as long as I live,*
> *and in your name I will lift up my hands.*
>
> PSALM 63:3–4

11 October

'Whatever happens, I'm not going to cry,' I tell myself sternly.

We've known that this day would arrive, and now it's here. The long preparation of the last few weeks is finally over, and boxes stuffed with food, clothing and study materials are piled high in the hall, waiting to be carried out to the car.

We cram everything into the car boot, and get in. A long drive lies ahead of us, and we're all feeling tired when we finally draw up at the campus where our youngest son will spend his first year at art college.

Here we go through the whole process again in reverse order, directed by a helpful student to a small room with breezeblock walls, the only decoration a long list of rules pinned to a cork board, beginning with 'No posters are to be attached to the walls with Blu-tack'.

'I'm glad it's got a view.' At least you can see hills and trees over the tops of the houses.

All the 'mother' thoughts are rushing through my head. 'Will he eat properly? Will he bother to cook, or is he just going to eat junk food? What about if he gets ill? Is he going to make friends? Will he like it here? What will the course be like?'

There are several other parents in the student flat, also helping their offspring move in, and from the look of their faces, I can see they're feeling it too.

'This is worse than going for a job interview,' says one of the mothers as we stack tins of soup, chopped tomatoes and baked beans in the cupboards, side by side.

I nod my head. 'Worse than going to the dentist, even.'

Even my husband is unnaturally quiet as he helps set up the computer on the desk.

'Well, we ought to be going,' he says finally, looking at his watch.

'OK, I'll walk down with you.'

The three of us walk slowly to where we've left the car.

Our tall son reaches over and gives us both a big hug. We hold on to each other, and I've broken my resolution. My eyes are wet.

'Love you, Mum. Love you, Dad.'

'Love you, too.'

We drive off and leave him standing there, looking after the car, waving.

✥

My husband and I have just joined the ranks of the 'empty nesters', and it's an unsettling change. From having a house full of teenagers and all that that involves—food disappearing at lightning speed from fridge and cupboards, piles of washing, and loud music—we are now rattling around in a house that suddenly seems empty, and far too quiet.

It's not that we didn't want him to go off and lead his own life— we did. But even when we know something is right, it can still be hard to get used to doing things a different way.

There's something in the human psyche that is resistant to change. Somehow the 'way we've always done things' seems far more appealing than doing something in a new way that lacks the comfort of familiarity.

Water in a stream needs to be constantly flowing to remain fresh and clean. If something blocks the flow, it is not long before the water becomes stagnant, an unpleasant green scum forming on its surface.

And yet sometimes it seems we prefer the static, the lack of movement—at least then we don't have to worry about where the current is taking us.

Even when we know it will do us good, change can still cause us problems. Jesus met a man at the pool of Bethesda who had been ill for 38 years—a very long time (John 5:2–15).

Normally we find people coming to Jesus and asking for healing, but it seems that in this case Jesus made the approach. His question to the sick man was an interesting one. 'Do you want to be made well?'

Surely the answer was obvious, wasn't it? Of course the man wanted to be well. Wouldn't anybody long for the suffering of 38 years to stop?

Yet sometimes we grow so used to our difficult circumstances that we almost get a perverse enjoyment out of them. Someone tells you, 'I haven't been to church since they treated me so badly'—but then you find out that the incident happened ten years ago! The flood of water has been dammed, and the supply is no longer fresh.

The sick man appeared to dodge the question. Instead of a plain 'Yes' or 'No', he told Jesus that he hadn't been healed because he had nobody to help him get into the pool in time, so that somebody else always got there first. Perhaps he had given up hope that his life could ever change, and his mat had become his security.

Change can be frightening. The sick man's life was centred on his disabilities, but if he was healed, he could no longer spend the whole day on his mat. He would have to fill his day with other activities—perhaps get a job.

It's strange that sometimes even though we don't enjoy the state we're in, we've gradually acclimatized to it, settled in it. After a while, we even forget how restrictive we originally found the situation. It's like a 'life corset', and it's amazing how quickly we get used to the way it restricts our breathing. In fact, we almost can't remember what it was like to breathe properly and deeply. We've learned to love the constriction, and find security in it.

When we've opted for the backwater lifestyle instead of adapting to change and growing, we often look back nostalgically to the way life used to be.

'Oh, I was so happy when the children were little. Now they've left home, my life is empty.'

'I preferred that church. God was moving so powerfully then.'

'I never really wanted to move. Even now, this just doesn't feel like home.'

Yet change with God is vibrant and exciting, just as freely running water energizes and brings life. We do not need to become casualties if we face the challenges of change with the strength that God so readily supplies.

'Who shall separate us from the love of Christ? Shall trouble or hardship or persecution or famine or nakedness or danger or sword? … No, in all these things we are more than conquerors through him who loved us' (Romans 8:35, 37).

Backwaters are safe, but don't be fooled—ultimately they are dead ends, going nowhere.

Get up off your mat. Break free of the corset. Allow the living water to flow past the blockages, sweeping them away.

'Get up! Pick up your mat and walk,' Jesus said to the sick man.

It's time to get moving again.

16 October

The sun is almost unbearable, beating through the dust-streaked windscreen of our small rented car. We've been exploring all morning—stopping off at a village here, a monastery there—and thought it would be cooler in the Troodos Mountains of Cyprus where we are on holiday.

I unscrew the lid of our almost empty plastic water bottle and hand it to Steve. He takes a swig, making a wry face. 'Almost the same temperature as outside.'

I take a taste too. 'Mmm, see what you mean.'

At least it's wet, even if it is unpleasantly warm, and it's important not to get dehydrated in these high temperatures.

Just then we see a signpost pointing down a road that branches off to the left. 'Paphos. Twenty kilometres.'

Steve slows the car. 'Twenty kilometres? That's much quicker than going back the way we've come. It'll be nearer sixty if we do that.'

We're both hot and tired. The thought of being able to shorten our journey and relax by the hotel swimming-pool is irresistible.

We turn off, and the first few miles flash by. We're only a little further on, however, when the tarmac peters out.

In its place is a chalky white surface, but we carry on undeterred. We've already encountered this several times elsewhere on the island, and, apart from being a bit bumpy, it's perfectly drivable.

Or so we think.

After a short while, the track begins to twist and climb. Steve is sweating and his knuckles whiten as he wrestles with the steering wheel. I stop looking out of the window—the sheer drop into the valley far below does nothing for my nerves.

We talk about turning back, but the thought of negotiating all those hairpin bends again is just too much. 'We must be over halfway by now,' mutters my husband. 'Surely the road can't get any worse.'

For the next forty minutes we endure a nightmare journey. My husband crashes through the gears, the car engine whining as the gradient gets steeper and steeper and steeper. I have visions of getting out to push, but we finally make it to the top—just!

Thank goodness, it's now downhill, although the road's surface is littered with huge pot-holes, and we have slowed almost to walking pace. Every bone and muscle in my body has been jarred and jounced as effectively as if I'd spent an hour in the gym.

Steve heaves a sigh of relief as the track levels out. We pass into a forested area, very pleasant after the exposed hillside we have just rattled through.

A green clearing opens out where a stream sparkles over its stony bed, and lush flowering shrubs and climbing plants provide splashes of vivid colour. A family is picnicking beside a sturdy white Landrover.

They look up in disbelief as we emerge from the trees in our tinny rattling vehicle, and then their faces break into radiant smiles of understanding.

One of them shouts, and waves his full wine glass to us in a toast as we judder along the ruts, leaving a trail of dust in our wake. 'Here comes the Engleesh!'

I slide lower into my seat, embarrassed, but it doesn't stop me hearing the chorus of whistles and cheers. 'The Engleesh! The Engleesh!' they laugh with delight as we bump agonizingly slowly past.

✥

Daniel had far more to cope with than just the problem of foreign road systems when Jerusalem fell into the hands of King Nebuchadnezzar, and he was taken off to Babylon, far away from his native land.

For Daniel, this was not a short-term option allowing him to return at a future date to the place where he had grown up. He had no choice at all in the matter. He was a captive, and from now on this would be his home.

It must have been hard as Daniel faced up to the challenges

of a different language, different clothes, unfamiliar foods, and customs that were nothing like the ones he had known before. Even Daniel's name was changed. The master of the palace called him Belteshazzar.

It would have been very easy to forget all about his former existence, and totally adopt the ways of the people he now lived among, but Daniel was determined to continue his walk as a child of God.

The first step he took does not seem a very great one to us (Daniel 1:8). It was just a matter of what he ate and drank—hardly worth bothering about, you might think.

'Who cares about something like that? Surely it's a bit trivial… and besides, the palace food looks absolutely delicious!'

Even this seemingly small choice carried an element of risk, for Daniel and his three friends had to be seen to be at least as fit and healthy as the other young men who would also serve in the court of the king. However, God honoured the four young Israelites, and they gained favour above the other young men in the group.

It's such seemingly insignificant stands that pave the way for later situations when we need to be able to hold our ground. Compromising on lesser issues may feel like the easier option, but all too often it's a slippery slope that can lead to a day when we find that somehow we've become so entangled, it's almost impossible to break free.

It's very hard then to stand up and say, 'I'm a Christian and I don't believe this is right', because we have already tolerated so many other things.

It was because Daniel was faithful in even the smallest matters that he was prepared for larger challenges, so that when it came to the biggest test of all—whether he would still pray to God or face the death penalty—he did not waver for an instant (Daniel 6:7–10). His whole life was already aligned to follow in God's paths.

We will not be thrown into a lions' den like Daniel, but because God's way is often so different from what is going on around us, we can sometimes face ridicule or even hostility just because we are Christians. Have you come across any of these viewpoints?

- Christians as 'goodie goodies' who never do anything wrong and, if they do, it is immediately pointed out to them, 'But I thought you were a Christian!'
- Christians as killjoys. They don't do anything fun, and they don't want anyone else to have fun either.
- Christians as loners. They stick to their own little group and don't mix with anyone else.

It's a huge challenge to live in the world and yet not succumb to the pressure to act like everyone else. How many times have you thought:

'Why on earth didn't I say something when they started to talk like that, or at least remove myself from the situation?'

'Why didn't I speak out, and give God's viewpoint on that controversial issue?'

'Why did I allow myself to get drawn in when I knew all the time what I was doing was wrong?'

The Bible challenges us to be 'salt' in our society. 'Why salt?' you might think. 'What a strange choice!'

Although salt is a humble substance, it is also powerful, for those minute grains change whatever they are added to. Salt permeates everything around it, and as a result the flavour of any dish with it in is radically improved.

Salt also has astringent and antiseptic properties, stinging when it gets into a cut. Although painful, this serves a very important function, for it is this quality that acts as a preservative, preventing the growth of bacteria that make food go rotten.

Daniel was clearly a person with 'salt' in his character. He kept his distinctiveness, and was never afraid to speak his mind when confronted by evil. He 'told it like it was'.

When Belshazzar took sacred vessels from the temple, and used them to drink wine, drunkenly praising other gods, Daniel did not hesitate to pronounce God's judgment, even though he knew it wasn't what the king wanted to hear (Daniel 5:1–30)! Wherever Daniel went, everything he did and said was seasoned with the presence of God.

Although some other substances, like sugar, may resemble it, you only need to taste salt to be sure what it is. There's no way you'll be confused, thinking, 'Could that be cinnamon, or perhaps nutmeg? I'm not quite certain.' It's immediately obvious.

What about us? Is it obvious that we're Christians, or are the edges a little blurred? Salt without flavour has no purpose. In fact, it can no longer be called salt. As Jesus said, 'It is no longer good for anything, except to be thrown out and trampled under foot' (Matthew 5:13).

Mark 9:50 ends with a curious phrase that sounds like a cookery instruction, but we need to take it seriously: 'Have salt in yourselves.'

Why? Because we are the 'salt of the earth' (Matthew 5:13), and if we are being salt, change around us is inevitable. People will begin to see and taste God.

Check your salt levels. Are they high enough to make a difference to those around you? If not, why not?

21 October

There seems to be an unwritten law that the more important it is to get to church on time on a Sunday, the more events conspire to make this an impossibility.

The things that can go wrong vary at different times of our lives. If you have a baby, Sunday will be the morning when the little darling is sick all over you, requiring a complete change of clothing.

Then, as children grow older, there's the whole military precision of the operation required to get parents plus children in the car on time, often involving raised voices and heightened blood pressure.

There are also multiple variations—you receive a phone call from chatty Great-aunt Agatha just as you are leaving, or the car engine that was running perfectly smoothly yesterday now refuses to start. The only factor they have in common is that they make you late!

In our church we have a new delaying mechanism—it's called picking up students. This Sunday morning I'm in charge of making coffee before the service, and Steve is leading worship, both activities needing an early start.

We're almost ready to go when the phone rings, and a voice that sounds half-asleep asks, 'Can I have a lift?'

'Yes, of course we'll pick you up, Tom,' says Steve. 'But it'll have to be on the early side. We're on coffee and worship today.'

'Right you are.'

We load up the car with guitar, music stand, amplifier and coffee box.

Picking up Tom doesn't start well. We have only recently moved to Exeter, and are still unfamiliar with the road systems. Although we know where we want to go, actually getting there is more complicated.

When we come to the third 'No Right Turn' in a row, my husband's knuckles tighten on the wheel.

'How on earth do we get to this place?'

Eventually we turn into Tom's road. Steve looks at his watch. Precious minutes have been lost, and we are beginning to feel the pressure.

We drive slowly down the long narrow road with cars parked either side. 'Can you see the number?'

'No, but he'll probably be waiting outside.'

But there's no sign of him, and when we see the house itself, there are no lights on downstairs.

We have to drive some way up the road before we can park. I hurry back to Tom's door, and press the grubby doorbell. I'm sure Tom will be straight out—he probably just hasn't seen the car.

Nobody comes. I press the bell again. Is it working?

At the third attempt, I hear a distant thudding of feet, steadily growing louder. A tall boy in a dressing-gown yanks open the door, looking rather grumpy at being disturbed from his Sunday morning lie-in.

I feel a bit guilty. 'Is Tom here, please?'

The boy yawns. 'No, he's gone to church.'

'Are you sure? He asked us to pick him up.'

'Hang on, I'll just go and look.'

After a few minutes he comes back to the door.

'He'll be down in a minute.'

Tom pops a tousled head over the banisters.

'Really sorry, Clare. I must've gone back to sleep.'

I go back to the car.

'Where is he?'

'Coming.'

'I'm supposed to be there at 9.45.'

'And I've got to get the kettles on, and the cups put out by ten,' I wail.

Eventually, Tom wanders out to the car, clutching two pieces of toast in one hand. 'Breakfast,' he explains as he clambers into the back seat.

'So, guys,' he says brightly, 'are we ready?'

✧

Few of us are good at waiting, and long queues in supermarkets, banks and at bus stops leave us fuming. We would like to cut out waiting altogether, and live in a perfect world where everything works like clockwork, but it just doesn't work like that in reality.

We may think we have our day mapped out, but all too often we end up with something totally different.

Life is similarly complex. Although we may have a very real sense of the direction we want our life to go in—goals, ambitions, even visions given by God—things rarely work out quite the way we expect.

Joseph certainly found that life was full of unexpected twists and turns. It started when he was 17, and God gave him two dreams (Genesis 37:5–9) that showed his brothers and his parents bowing before him. Young and immature, Joseph could not resist bragging about his dreams—an unwise decision that made him even more unpopular with his already jealous brothers.

Determined not to put up with such a spoilt brat, they were at first tempted to kill him, but instead sold him to some Midianite traders, who then sold him on to Potiphar, the captain of Pharaoh's guard in Egypt.

Joseph suffered the devastating blow of losing his home and family, but 'The Lord was with Joseph and he prospered' (39:2).

Things were going well again for Joseph. Potiphar trusted him, and made him overseer over his house and possessions, but unfortunately Potiphar's wife had also taken a shine to the handsome young man.

She wanted Joseph to become her lover, but he resisted all her advances. 'How then could I do such a wicked thing and sin against God?' (39:9).

She would not give up, however. One day she tried to corner him in the bedroom, but Joseph fled rather than give in to sin, leaving his cloak in her hand.

How hard it must have been, then, to be unjustly accused and thrown into prison when he had done nothing wrong! Joseph must have wondered what was going on: 'I have tried to do what is right, and yet here I am suffering.' Have you ever felt like that?

The downturn in his fortunes had not been Joseph's fault. He could have become bitter and blamed God, but he did not, and once again 'the Lord was with him; he showed him kindness and granted him favour in the eyes of the prison warder' (v. 21).

Prison felt very far away from the dreams that Joseph had had as a boy, but God was still with him in the depths of the prison: 'the Lord was with Joseph and gave him success in whatever he did' (v. 23).

Joseph had changed a lot from the boastful youth full of his own importance—he was a man who had learned to lean on God. When two frightened prisoners had troubling dreams, he knew where to find help: 'Do not interpretations belong to God?' (40:8).

With God's help, Joseph interpreted their dreams, and when the chief cupbearer walked free to be reinstated into his royal position, Joseph probably thought that, with a friend in high places, his own release could not be far away.

But days, weeks and months passed. One year went by, and then another, and Joseph was still in prison, still waiting, still putting his trust in God, although his circumstances seemingly remained as bad as ever.

It's not always easy to understand the whole process of waiting. Joseph had continually behaved righteously, no matter where he found himself, but it seemed to have got him nowhere.

Do you think that Joseph sometimes recalled his boyhood visions, and wondered if he had got it wrong? Do you think he was tempted to feel that God had let him down? Nothing in his dreams had suggested slavery and a prison. Surely this couldn't be part of God's plan for his life, could it?

Joseph did not give up on God. Finally, after two years, the cupbearer remembered him when Egypt's magicians and wise men failed to interpret Pharaoh's dreams. Joseph refused to take any credit himself for interpreting dreams, but told Pharaoh, 'I cannot do it… but God will give Pharaoh the answer he desires' (41:16).

Rewarded by Pharaoh with power and position, the day came when, as in his boyhood dreams, his brothers bowed before him—seeking grain in time of famine. Joseph could have paid them back for what they had done to him, but he did not.

Instead he saw God's hand at work in every part of his life, both good and bad:

'It was to save lives that God sent me ahead of you' (45:5).

'So then, it was not you who sent me here, but God' (v. 8).

The waiting process is difficult, and can lead to disillusionment and frustration. When we feel stuck, it is only too easy to become bitter and conclude that God is no longer interested in us or in our situation.

But there is another way, the Joseph approach—seeing God's hand at work whatever happens to us, and knowing that everything is part of God's design for our life.

- The best coffee is not instant.
- The best wine is not made from grapes that have had little time to ferment.
- The best fruit is not torn from the tree before it is fully formed, but has ripened slowly on the branch, its delicious taste compounded by wind, rain showers and sunshine.

Waiting need not be wasted time, but precious time that does a work of God in our lives, if we allow him to have his perfect way within us.

> *I wait for the Lord, my soul waits,*
> *and in his word I put my hope.*
> *My soul waits for the Lord*
> *more than watchmen wait for the morning,*
> *more than watchmen wait for the morning.*
>
> PSALM 130:5–6

25 October

The phone's ringing. Who on earth can it be at this early hour? I stumble out of bed to answer it.

It's Tony, Mum's husband. Apparently, she's been taken into hospital again, and he hasn't been able to go with her in the ambulance. 'Can you ring the hospital and find out what's going on?'

'No cause for concern,' says the doctor when I get through. 'We'll be sending her home soon. She's giving me a hard time because I can't find a vein to take blood. Problem is, she's tough as an old boot, aren't you, Rosie?'

I can hear Mum laughing in the background, and, reassured, I put the phone down.

Everything's fine, but somehow I just can't settle. I try to get on with my work, but it's impossible to concentrate. At last I give up.

'I'm going to the hospital,' I say to Steve.

'But the doctor said there was no need.'

'I know, but I keep getting this feeling I should be there.'

My husband looks at me, and picks up the car keys. 'Let's go, then.'

❖

It's not the first time I've had this feeling. I've even got a name for it—the 'niggle of the Spirit'. You may have experienced the same thing, an overwhelming compulsion to phone someone, drop them a line, or simply turn up on their doorstep. This is what I was experiencing now—a strong urgency: 'Go to the hospital.'

Whenever I've ignored such 'feelings', perhaps because I've been too busy or too tired or had something I'd rather be doing,

I've always wished in retrospect that I'd heeded that 'still, small voice'.

The trouble is that we're not naturally tuned into that frequency. We have to learn to listen, and it's not easy when there's so much going on to distract us.

If we're not careful, we can dismiss what God is saying to us, thinking that we're imagining it, or even put off responding to some more convenient time... and then, of course, we never actually get round to it.

That's another thing about God's voice. He often seems to speak when we're right in the middle of something else that we'd really rather not interrupt.

And he doesn't confine himself to reasonable hours, either. How many of us have been woken up with an urge to pray for something or someone in the early hours of the morning?

So what happens then? Do we burrow deeper into our nice cosy bed, excusing ourselves: 'Well, you know how cross I get with the family if I don't get enough rest?'

Or do we feel we're doing our bit by mumbling a few quick words before dozing off again? After all, God understands, doesn't he? 'You know I can't concentrate at this time of night, Lord. I'll pray much better in the morning.'

Or do we react with simple obedience like Samuel? God spoke to him in the middle of the night (1 Samuel 3:1–18) not just once, but three times.

The Mystery of the Voice in the Night

Scene 1

Samuel, in bed, hears someone calling his name. He assumes that old Eli the priest needs something, but when Samuel gets up and runs to his master, Eli tells him to go back to bed.

Samuel does as he's told, puzzled. Eli says he didn't call his name, and yet Samuel is sure he heard a voice. Perhaps it was the cheese he ate at supper giving him vivid dreams? Samuel dozes off.

Scene 2

(Some time later) Samuel hears his name being called again, but once more Eli sends him away. Samuel wonders what is going on.

Scene 3

(Some time even later) The voice calls 'Samuel' again. Samuel is tempted to ignore it, roll over and go back to sleep—he's already got up twice. Fortunately, our hero responds for the third time.

Eli the priest has been working out the clues. 'It's not me calling you. It's God.' The mystery is solved.

Hearing the word of God was rare in Samuel's time, and in our own age of cynicism and materialism, the idea of God speaking to everyday men and women is often greeted with derision. 'You must be joking!'

When we first sense God's prompting, we too can be tempted to dismiss it. 'Oh no, that couldn't possibly be God—that's just me.'

Or perhaps we are assailed by doubts. 'Am I imagining it, or is it really God?'

God always speaks to us for a purpose, sometimes to encourage us, sometimes to impress on us something we need to do, or attitudes we need to change. Sadly, we can shut our ears to what God is saying to us, although we do so at our peril.

It's a bit like children who, if they are in the middle of an absorbing game, become suddenly deaf when you ask them to come in and wash their hands before tea.

Selective hearing is another common problem—hearing when

God is telling us to do something we want to do, but ignoring him if it's something we struggle with.

'Make friends with that difficult neighbour.'

'Forgive that person who really hurt you.'

Ouch! Surely God can't mean me to do that.

Samuel could have ignored the voice calling him, but he would never have developed into the man of God that he later became. Once you have begun a conversation with God, it leaves you hungry to hear more.

Moments when God speaks to us are precious. How sad if we ignore him, or rush off without really listening to what he has to say! I was so glad I listened, for by the time I reached the hospital, things had taken a turn for the worse and Mum was fighting for her life.

For me, it was a word of urgency: 'Go to the hospital.' For you, it might be a prompting to get involved with others in your family, church, work or neighbourhood.

'Ring Jane. She needs a word of encouragement.'

'Give Angie a love gift. I want you to demonstrate my generosity.'

When we come into God's presence we often fill the time with a long list of our concerns. However, God created us with one mouth, but two ears. Do you think he was trying to tell us something?

Good listeners are hard to find, but good spiritual listeners, attuned to God's voice, are even rarer and more precious.

Do you want to hear God?

Learn to be a good listener like Samuel.

'Here I am, Lord. I'm listening. I'm available.'

27 October

We've been waiting for what seems like hours in the hospital waiting-room before the doctor comes, and when he does, it's not good news. Mum has slipped into deep unconsciousness, and they don't expect her to last the night.

It's hard to take the news in. The nurse leaves us alone with a phone so that we can call the rest of the family. My brother in London can't make it until the morning, as his wife is away and his little boy is fast asleep. 'Come as soon as you can,' I urge him.

Mum is heavily sedated, and we take turns sitting by her, holding her hand. 'Talk to her,' says the nurse. 'She may be able to hear you. Hearing's the last thing to go.'

Amazingly, Mum is still alive when morning comes. I think I see her eyelids flicker as though she is trying to open them, but the doctor says it's a common reflex.

Mum has always been one for drama, but today even she surpasses herself. When the doctor comes to check on her during his ward round, she suddenly sits up and exclaims, 'Oh, my dears—I hope I haven't been causing any trouble.'

I think she almost gives the doctor a heart attack. He certainly looks as white as a sheet!

Through the remainder of the day, all five children, their spouses, Mum's husband Tony, and several of the grandchildren gather around her bed. It's a wonderful family time, and we feel such relief.

We are sure that having survived this crisis, she will pull through, and that all she needs now is plenty of rest and loving care to regain her strength and be able to go back home.

She has quite a good night, but the following day she's obviously worn out from being the life and soul of the party—her favourite role. It's plain that what Mum needs more than anything else is peace and quiet.

The last to go, I don't feel good about leaving her on her own. 'Go and have a break for a few hours,' encourages the nurse. 'Ring back later, and we'll let you know how she's doing.'

I'm far too tired to cook, so we go out to a local pub for some food. Halfway through, we get a call. Mum's heart has arrested. 'Why, why did I leave her?' I sob as our youngest son drives me to the hospital while Steve rushes over to collect Tony.

I'm afraid she will be dead when we get there, but once again she has bounced back. However, the doctor tells us gravely that there is no hope. The kindest thing now is not to keep the heart beating artificially any more. He is switching the machine off.

'You're going to have to put your trust in God now, Rosie,' says Steve. 'I do,' Mum replies softly. We hold her hand and gently stroke her head, telling her that we love her as her life ebbs slowly away. Then she is gone.

❖

It's hard to watch someone die and to walk with them through their last moments, but it is a privilege too. Nowadays, death has become almost as much a taboo subject as sex was to the Victorians.

In the past, death was far more a natural part of life as the elderly lived out their remaining years in the midst of their families. Today, it seems to be something that we're not really prepared for, and we act as if it's something that's never going to happen. But we are fooling ourselves—death is where we are headed, every single one of us.

I love the story of the thief who met Jesus at the cross (Luke 23:32–43). He probably wasn't a very nice man. He hadn't done much good—he'd lied and cheated and robbed his way through a life that was wretched and mean. Where others might have helped an old lady across the road, he was more likely to pinch her purse.

Now he was facing a brutal death, he couldn't say he didn't

deserve it. He didn't try to defend himself, saying, 'What have I done to die like this?' He knew he'd done plenty of cruel and selfish acts.

The thief knew he was a bad man. He knew just as certainly that the man being executed beside him was a good man, and possibly something more than that. People whispered that this Jesus was the Son of God and the promised Saviour of Israel. Could it be true? Was it possible? Deep within him, hope flickered.

One part of him argued fiercely: 'You're deluding yourself. You've messed up your whole life and, even if this Jesus is the Saviour, why should he be interested in you? You've not been good. Everything in your life has been rotten.'

On the other side of Jesus was another criminal, but his approach was entirely different. The second thief cursed and swore, and even as he faced death he shook his fist at it.

He too had heard the rumours about the man Jesus, but they affected him very little. Saviour? So what? He had lived his whole life the way he wanted to live it, and he was going to die the same way he had lived, raging against the system. He didn't need anyone, and certainly not a Saviour.

The first thief bowed his head. He had no illusions about himself. He knew there was no way he deserved a place in heaven, but even as his life was running out, he knew that a choice lay before him.

The choice was simple.

Do you want to be with Jesus?

Or without him?'

'Jesus, remember me when you come into your kingdom' (v. 42).

Jesus' response is beautiful. He doesn't say, 'Don't you realize how many sins you've clocked up? What makes you think there's a place in heaven for someone like you?' or 'Well, you've done a lot of bad things, so you'll have to go on a "Fit for Heaven" course first.'

Jesus responds in love: 'I tell you the truth, today you will be with me in paradise' (v. 43).

Imagine how, even though his body was racked with pain, the first thief must have felt an incredible sense of peace dawn in his soul. He was going to be in paradise, and not only that, his companion would be Jesus himself. Fear of death vanished with the prospect of such joy before him.

Defeating death was a major part of God's plan when Jesus went to the cross for us, as we read in one of the most famous verses in the Bible: 'For God so loved the world that he gave his one and only Son, that whoever believes in him shall not perish but have eternal life' (John 3:16).

For those who have turned to Jesus, death is no longer something to fear, but simply a doorway through which we pass to run into the open arms of Jesus.

WINTER

For I am convinced that neither death nor life, neither angels nor demons, neither the present nor the future, nor any powers, neither height nor depth, nor anything else in all creation, will be able to separate us from the love of God that is in Christ Jesus our Lord.
ROMANS 8:38–39

5 November

I walk around the bedroom, picking up clothes and putting them back into the wardrobe. My husband has just gone off to a conference in London, and won't be back for a few days. Time to catch up on that book I've been planning to finish for weeks.

I've just finished lunch when the phone rings.

'Hi, Mum.' It's our eldest son, Dave. 'I thought you might be lonely, so I'm coming down to keep you company.'

'That's very thoughtful. How nice.'

'A few friends are coming too—I'm taking them over to Tar Barrels.'

Tar Barrels is an annual local event where—yes—flaming tar barrels are carried through the streets in an old tradition that has so far somehow escaped health and safety regulations. It's enormous fun, and very exciting.

'How many friends?' I say, mentally checking out the contents of the freezer.

'Only three,' he says breezily.

'And when are you coming?'

'Oh, we've already started.'

Food and bedding for four extra people involves a quick dash to the shops for giant pizzas and other goodies, and a hunt for sleeping bags and pillows, just finished when they arrive on the doorstep.

Dinner is a noisy, sociable affair with much talking and laughter. Soon afterwards they set out for the evening, leaving the car in the drive.

'We won't drink and drive, Mum, don't worry, and we'll get a taxi back. Don't wait up.'

Later, heavy rain beats against the windows. 'Hope they're in the warm,' I think as I drop off to sleep.

My dream is interrupted by a persistent sound. I surface with a groan. The phone's ringing downstairs. I stumble out of bed.

'Yes?'

Blearily, I notice the kitchen clock. It's 1.30 am.

'Mum, I'm really sorry. We can't get a taxi—we've started to walk back, but it's raining, and the girls are freezing. Could you…?'

'Just give me time to get dressed. I'll be about twenty minutes.'

I scramble into warm clothes and head out to the car. It's dark and very wet, and I drive carefully on the narrow winding roads.

Eventually my headlights pick them out, a forlorn bunch walking doggedly along, heads down. They climb thankfully into the car, water dripping from their clothing, shoes squelching.

'Goodness, you couldn't get much wetter if you'd had a shower!'

Back home, I root out thick woolly jumpers and make some hot soup. Three in the morning, and it's a homely scene with us all sitting round the table, clutching mugs of tea.

Yawning, I say goodnight.

'Thanks, Mum.' My tall son gives me a hug.

What a night!

✢

We'll do things for our families that we don't generally do for anyone else.

'Can you lend me some money, Dad?' and we reach into our pockets.

'My jeans need mending. Is there any chance you can fix them before Saturday as I want to wear them to Ben's party?' Out come the needle and thread.

Family is all about looking out for each other. When we feel low or have something to celebrate, our close family are often the first to know.

Of course, families have their rough edges. Sometimes we fall out and sometimes we can't stand each other, but when we need each other, the family is always there, providing security and acceptance.

I think of all the times when we as a family have supported each other, helping to move house, when a new baby has arrived, in hospital vigils, and in glorious family celebrations. As family, we are committed to one another, come what may.

As Christians, we belong to another family too—God's family. Look in the Bible, and you will see that this church family is described in terms of the closest relationships—fathers, mothers, brothers, sisters and children.

'For in Christ Jesus I became your father through the gospel' (Paul in 1 Corinthians 4:15).

'Timothy, my son whom I love, who is faithful in the Lord' (1 Corinthians 4:17).

'I commend to you our sister Phoebe' (Romans 16:1).

'Greet Rufus, chosen in the Lord, and his mother, who has been a mother to me, too' (Romans 16:13).

'He is a dear brother, a faithful minister and fellow servant in the Lord' (Paul speaking of Tychicus in Colossians 4:7).

'As a son with his father he has served with me in the work of the gospel' (Paul speaking of Timothy in Philippians 2:22).

'To Apphia our sister' (Philemon 2).

'My dear children…' (1 John 2:1).

Over and over again the readers of the New Testament letters are addressed as 'brothers and sisters' (for example, 1 Corinthians 1:10, 11, 26, NRSV).

Of course, families can be prone to squabbles.

'It's not fair—it's my turn now.'

'Mum, he pushed me.'

'Why can't I join in?'

'I want one too!'

But although family members may try our patience at times, such storms are only temporary. The relationship is still strong—you are there for them, and they are there for you. My family know that if they need me in a time of crisis, they only have to pick up the phone and I will get there if I possibly can.

Church families too are not immune from friction.

'Why can't they see things the way I do?'

'She hurt me when she said that.'

'I'm not sitting by him.'

But God wants us to display the same commitment and caring attitude towards our brothers and sisters in Christ that we would towards our own immediate family.

Sometimes we would much prefer a more distant relationship. We would rather be an uncle, an aunt or a cousin, happy for an occasional get-together, so long as not too much contact is involved.

God wants more than that. He wants fathers who will lead well, giving a righteous example of walking with God, and mothers who will selflessly love and encourage. He wants daughters who will seek to grow up into godliness, and sons who will be on fire for God. He wants children who are obedient and quick to learn, not stubborn and resistant.

Belonging to the family of God is an amazing privilege. You can travel to the next town, or hundreds of miles to another country, and still find a feeling of kinship, an immediate closeness, with people you've never met before. The reason is simple—they're part of the same family!

12 November

We had fond memories of this place and I was really looking forward to our meal out. We'd celebrated a number of our anniversaries here and loved the atmosphere.

This evening, though, was to be an experience of an altogether different kind.

'Where is everybody?' I whispered to Steve.

Normally the place was packed, but tonight it was virtually empty. We soon found out why.

We stood there waiting for the spotty young man who was excavating his fingernails with a cocktail stick to notice us.

'Hmmph.' My husband cleared his throat. When that got no response, he coughed several times with increasing loudness.

The youth ambled over, cocktail stick still clutched in his hand. He tried to direct us to a table right by the toilets, and seemed to take it personally when we asked for a window table instead.

'Chicken… off, so is the salmon.' He slapped a stained menu grumpily in front of us.

We looked at each other. Things were not going well.

We chose what we wanted to eat, and after a gap of about ten minutes looked around for our waiter.

It wasn't because he was over-busy that he hadn't come to our table yet. In fact he was propped against the doorway into the kitchen, looking as if he could barely keep his eyes open.

Eventually he seemed to jerk awake, and stumbled over to take our order.

'Nice weather today,' I smiled.

He looked at me as if I was from another planet.

'S'all right.'

He shuffled off, and we waited some more.

'Do you think they're growing the potatoes from scratch?' said my hungry husband.

'Sssh.'

Bored Youth plonked two plates in front of us.

'Nnsss?' Bored Youth made a noise like a bee buzzing.

'Pardon?'

'ANY SAUCES?'

'Oh, yes, could we have some mustard, please?'

'I don't think that was the right answer,' I said as Bored Youth scowled and clomped heavily back into the kitchen, reappearing with a small plastic sachet.

Steve opened it and tried to eke out the minuscule contents over his shrivelled steak.

'I'm sure they used to have the real thing here.'

Romance was finding it hard going, and so were our jaws as we chomped our way through the tough meat. All the way through our meal, Bored Youth didn't smile once.

We decided to leave dessert, and drank our bitter coffee hurriedly. It definitely wasn't a place where you felt like lingering.

'Service isn't included,' said the waiter as he handed us the bill.

'It certainly isn't,' muttered my husband.

✢

The way we serve a person says a lot about where we are coming from. Let's face it, the whole idea of serving is something we tend to struggle with in today's world. Everyone would rather be served than be a server, because the server is seen as inferior.

After all, what life does a servant have? A servant must put the needs of the one he serves first, no matter how tired, hungry or even sick the servant is.

And what about job satisfaction? Who do you notice most—the person who puts out the seats or the speaker who fills them?

Exactly. No wonder very few people, when asked what they want to do in church, put 'servant' at the top of their list.

Yet Jesus sees servants very differently. In fact, he classes himself among them.

Answer this question. In a room, you have the Son of God and an uneducated fisherman with a tendency to lose his temper. Who should serve whom?

Peter knew what he thought. 'You will never wash my feet!' (John 13:8, NRSV) he cries in horror as Jesus approaches him with a bowl of water and a towel. How can it be right for the Son of God to kneel before him and wash the dust and grime from his hard, calloused skin?

For Jesus, though, that is why he is here: 'But I am among you as one who serves' (Luke 22:27); 'the Son of Man did not come to be served, but to serve' (Matthew 20:28).

If we are following Jesus, serving is part of our Christian walk, not an optional extra. So how are we doing?

Do we see serving as a chore, something to be got through with gritted teeth as quickly as possible? 'Oh no, they've put me on the coffee rota again!'

Serving grudgingly is a pain both for the server and the person being served, no matter how efficiently the task is performed.

The difference between graceless service, and service that truly blesses the receiver, is simply one of attitude.

The one says, 'I'm doing this because I must.' The other says, 'I'm doing this because I can.'

There is no question that serving requires discipline. It does not come naturally, for we have to learn to set aside our sense of self-importance, the part of us that constantly demands attention: 'Me first! Me first!'

Instead we look to Jesus.

He did not travel the 'Me first!' route.

Jesus was all 'You first!'

He said it to his Father constantly: 'Yet not my will, but yours be done' (Luke 22:42).

He said it to us when he died in our place on the cross: 'You first! You first!'

When we serve, we may feel discouraged because those we serve take what we do for granted, or our serving may even go unnoticed altogether.

But then that's not why we do it. We do it simply because we are trying to follow in the steps of the greatest servant who ever lived. And we too are learning to say, more and more, not 'Me first!' but 'You first!'

Not our will, but yours, Lord—whatever it takes.

18 November

I go from the sitting-room to the kitchen, and look among the piles of papers stacked on the coffee table, and the unpaid bills on top of the breadbin.

I look beside the telephone, and on the bureau, and I check our bedside cupboards. I even look in the bathroom in case I took them off while I was brushing my teeth, but they're not there either.

Now I have glasses, I also have a new problem—trying to remember where I put them the night before.

It's a small thing, but on this Monday morning it's just the last straw. It seems that now even inanimate objects are conspiring against me. For the last few weeks I've been struggling to set aside time to work on this book, and now, when I finally have a few free hours, I can't find my glasses.

Every month I've thought, 'This month will be easier. This time I'll really manage to get lots done', but it just hasn't worked out like that. Life is hectic at the moment, and although much of what is happening is really good and exciting, I'm beginning to feel like margarine that has been thinly scraped over too much bread.

I've been getting steadily more and more panicky as time has continued to march forward, and I still have little or nothing to show for it. Like a hamster going round and round on its wheel, my last thought before going to sleep, 'But what on earth shall I write?' is echoed by my first thought on waking, 'But what on earth shall I write?' My mind is a blank, and my prayers are bouncing off the ceiling.

'Lord,' I say in desperation, 'If something doesn't happen, I'm going to have a nervous breakdown RIGHT NOW! I can't do it. You've picked the wrong person.'

It's one of those 'Are you in this, God?' moments. What was I thinking of when I took this on? Surely if God wanted me to do it, I wouldn't be finding it so difficult. Have I got it wrong?

> To be honest, I feel like just walking away. I mean, it's not that important, is it? God will forgive me if I give up. I know you want me to, Lord, but you don't know how difficult it is for me.

✢

Sometimes we get bogged down when a task seems too big for us. We look at it, and we just can't believe that we're equipped for the task.

When Jesus gave Simon a new name, Peter, it was a part of his new job description. Peter means 'rock', and the burly fisherman was to be the rock on which the new church would be founded. First of all, though, there was a big problem to overcome—the weakness of Peter's own character.

Peter was often very far from rock-like in his behaviour, wavering from boastful confidence, 'Of course, I will never betray you, Lord' to utter denial, 'No, I can definitely say I know absolutely nothing about this man. I've never seen him before in my life' (Mark 14:29, 71).

I wonder how Peter felt when Jesus turned and looked at him after his failure to stand by his Lord. Perhaps he desperately wanted to excuse himself: 'You knew what I was like, Jesus. I can't do what you are asking me to—I'm not capable of it.'

Of course Peter couldn't, but Jesus is the great enabler who makes it possible for us to do things that are far beyond our natural abilities, things that we know we can achieve only with God's help.

However, although God does have a special work or even works for each one of us to do, it's up to me whether I choose to run with it, or turn my back and go my own way. Nobody is going to force me to do anything—that is not God's way.

Sometimes we get very confused about what exactly is God's work. It's very easy to see the importance of 'full-time' Christian work, but then we look at what we're doing and we wonder whether there's any value in it at all.

Separating the squabbles of two under-fives day after day—

what's good about that? But actually, carefully nurturing children and training them in godly ways is very important in God's eyes.

A friend of ours spent a large proportion of his life waiting for God's 'special job', but it was only after a number of years that he realized he was already doing it, and that his current job *was* God's work for him.

At other times we push the boat out and seek to do something challenging for God, only to lose confidence in our sense of calling when we face difficult circumstances. Before we know it, we're in deep trouble.

Even if we have already experienced a number of situations where we've felt God's hand strongly guiding us, we are still not immune to storms which can affect our position in God and knock us off course.

Some of Jesus' disciples knew a great deal about life on the water, but the storm that hit them one night was something totally out of their experience. Yes, of course they'd seen wind and waves before, but not like this. They simply couldn't cope (Mark 4:35–41).

Although they knew that they were doing what Jesus wanted them to do, and that he was with them, it didn't stop them panicking. Even with Jesus in the boat, the disciples were still deeply afraid. 'Teacher, don't you care if we drown?' (v. 38).

Jesus spoke to the stormy seas and the roaring winds, and to the tumult in his disciples' spirit: 'Lord, we can't cope with this situation. We're totally out of our depth.'

'Quiet! Be still!' are the words of Jesus, and then, 'Why are you so afraid? Do you still have no faith?' (vv. 39–40).

Have we faith that Jesus has called us to what we are doing? Have we such a strong faith that when our boat is rocked, we will not abandon ship or turn back to the shore?

The disciples were in danger of being swamped beneath the waves because they had lost their focus. They should have looked straight to Jesus when trouble hit, but instead their minds were filled with fear because of the raging storm around them.

If we are in danger of being overwhelmed, if tides of conflict and distraction are swamping our boat, we must get our focus right on Jesus, nowhere else.

When the task seems far beyond us, we take heart because Jesus will never call us to something without equipping us for it. Philippians 1:6 reads, '[I am] confident of this, that he who began a good work in you will carry it on to completion until the day of Christ Jesus.'

We may at times feel underqualified, and it's perfectly natural to feel a twinge of fright as we go out into deeper waters than we've yet experienced, but we must not forget that we're not alone in the boat. Feel the fear and do it anyway! What we do, we do for God.

23 November

My Auntie Val said to me today, 'Of course, you must always remember that a little bit of Rosie lives on in each of you.'

It was such a comforting thing to say, for the more I think about it, the more I realize that it is true. Mum has left a legacy that she has passed down to her five children.

- Her quirky sense of humour.
- Her love of growing things: when we were growing up, meals were often put on hold while Mum just 'cleared these last few weeds'—except that the 'last few' were often, in fact, a whole flower border!
- Her ability to lose herself in a book, oblivious to everything else, caught up in the thrill of a good story.
- Her interest in those around her: Put Mum on a bus and by the time she got off she'd have made at least three new friends.
- An aversion to housework: Mum would have agreed wholeheartedly with the maxim that 'life is too short to stuff a mushroom'!

At different times I catch myself saying something and think, 'That was a very "Mum" thing to say.' Or I do some simple action, perhaps making one of Mum's special liver, bacon and onion pies, and it will suddenly strike me, as I fold the pastry over to enclose the filling, 'I remember Mum doing it like this— I'm doing it the way she showed me.'

❖

Some of our family characteristics are physical—certain facial features that can be traced back through the generations. We have a photograph of our oldest son as a baby (with almost no hair) sitting on Grandad's lap (who also has virtually no hair), and the family likeness is staggering.

My husband, being a scientist, likes to put it all down to genes, but is it? Is there a gene for a certain way of laughing, or for that unfortunate sense of humour that tends to come into its own at the most inappropriate moments—in very serious meetings, for example?

When Steve and I first started dating, his sister immediately noticed a small but subtle change in his behaviour. He started to raise his eyebrows, something none of his family did, but that my family do all the time to express a whole variety of emotions—surprise, disbelief, shock: 'No, really…!'

When we spend a lot of time with someone, it is inevitable that something of them will rub off on us—that's human nature.

And if we spend time in God's presence, something of him will be absorbed into our lives—that's godly nature.

Although Jesus was the Son of God, he did not choose to live on some lofty plane where he rarely, if ever, associated with his followers. That was not Jesus' way. He lived out his whole life in the closest, most intimate contact with his disciples.

- They saw him as he marvelled at the faith of a Roman centurion (Matthew 8:10).
- They saw him filled with joy when they returned from a successful preaching mission and shared how they had put what he had taught them into practice (Luke 10:17–20).
- They saw him weep over a Jerusalem that still could not recognize its Saviour, even when he lived and walked among them (Luke 19:41–42).
- They saw him angry with the religious leaders of the time who got bogged down in rules and regulations, instead of leading the people into God's presence (Matthew 23:23).

- They saw how he related to people that everyone else considered outcasts—tax collectors, lepers, foreigners, prostitutes (Mark 2:15; Luke 5:13; 7:39; John 4:7).
- They saw how he relied on his Father for everything (John 5:19).

And little by little, the disciples began to change, becoming less like the old Peter, John, Andrew and James, and more like Jesus.

And maybe sometimes James would overhear Andrew say something, and think, 'Wow, that's the sort of thing Jesus would say!'

Or Peter would react not with his customary brusque attitude, but with the acceptance that he was learning to give to those he would normally have had nothing to do with—Jesus shining through a fisherman who was definitely not known for his tact and sensitivity.

The same is true of us. As we spend time with Jesus each day, we will become more and more like him.

'Do you not realize that Christ Jesus is in you?' says 2 Corinthians 13:5. It's an awesome thought.

When you go to college and open your books to study, when you share a cup of coffee at work with your colleagues, or spend time with a friend or neighbour, it's not just you who's in that place. It's a little bit of Jesus too.

1 December

Something taps me on the shoulder. I turn round to see the unnerving sight of my grinning husband brandishing a silvery glitter-studded wand.

'Behold the tooth fairy!'

'The tooth fairy has a beard?'

'Why not? Equal opportunities, and all that.'

'I doubt it. Where on earth did you get that?'

'Found it in the alleyway when I was cycling up. And this.' He puts a navy school rucksack on the table.

'At first I thought it had been thrown away, but then I saw an open purse and pencil case further along. It's obviously stolen, but there's an address and phone number. I'll ring now to let them know it's been found.'

He spends several minutes explaining the situation on the phone, and then giving directions to our house. Soon afterwards the owner of the bag, Sophie, and her mum, Jenny, turn up, and we walk down the alley to see if we can find anything else.

'I accidentally left the car door unlocked when we went to the dentist,' Jenny explains. 'Normally our dog barks like mad if anyone comes near the car, but for some reason she didn't.'

We carry on chatting, and somehow the topic of church comes up. It turns out that Jenny is a Christian too. Not only that, but she's looking for a church, and lives not far away from the one we go to.

'I have heard of it,' she says, 'and a friend told me I should go and have a look, but I didn't feel I knew anybody, so I've been putting it off.'

'Well, you've met us now—we'll look out for you if you want to come along.'

We exchange phone numbers, and say a warm goodbye.

'How strange,' Jenny says. 'Meeting you like this because of a stolen bag.'

✣

Strange, or just another example of the way God intervenes in everyday life—another of his 'divine appointments' when seemingly random events work together?

It could so easily have been different. We might not have talked about church or Christianity at all, and we would have walked away from one another none the wiser—perhaps thought, 'Yes, they were nice people', but no more than that.

These are 'God-opportunities'—the chance to make connections, sometimes encouraging encounters with other Christians, sometimes being a link in the chain that eventually brings someone to Christ. But the connection has to be made first. Sparks cannot fly if the flint doesn't meet the stone.

It's not always easy, I have to say—far from it. In fact, I often find it hard to introduce God, or the fact that I'm a Christian, naturally into conversation.

Sometimes I imagine I have an alter ego: 'Charismatic Clare'. Charismatic Clare is the sort of Christian who will do something quite ordinary like going to the shops, and God will use her powerfully. Stand her in a queue, and she won't be thinking about how lamb has gone up in price, or what to cook for dinner later. Instead, a depressed-looking shop assistant will just happen to confide in her. 'There's no purpose to my life,' moans the miserable girl.

Gently, but persuasively, Charismatic Clare doesn't hesitate, sharing a few select Bible verses that (of course) she knows by heart. The girl's whole expression changes, and five minutes later she's given her life to the Lord. Charismatic Clare goes off rejoicing for a well-earned coffee.

If only! My experience tends to be more a saga of missed opportunities, kicking myself: 'Why on earth didn't I say something?'

I'm glad that I'm not the only one. Moses, for example, felt that he was too tongue-tied to communicate God's commands to the great Pharaoh, and, initially at least, relied on his more vocal brother Aaron to do the talking (Exodus 4:10–16).

In Acts 9, Ananias, a disciple in Damascus, also struggled with a situation where he knew that God wanted him to meet up with somebody and share his faith as a Christian.

You can understand Ananias' reluctance, for the name of the man God wanted him to talk to was hated and feared by Christians everywhere. Saul of Tarsus had the blood of so many believers on his hands. He was relentless in his persecution, and showed no mercy to those he caught.

Ananias couldn't help wondering if God really meant the same Saul. He tentatively reminded God of Saul of Tarsus' fearsome reputation: 'Lord, I have heard many reports about this man and all the harm he has done to your saints in Jerusalem. And he has come here with authority from the chief priests to arrest all who call on your name' (vv. 13–14).

Saul—that man of blood. Surely God would have nothing to do with this man of violence who so blatantly denied the Lordship of Jesus Christ. Ananias hoped he had misunderstood God. After all, if even half the stories told about Saul were true, he would be risking his life by going to see him. Images of imprisonment, torture and death filled his mind. He was scared. Please let it be some other Saul!

It was no mistake, however. He heard God's voice again: 'Go! This man is my chosen instrument to carry my name before the Gentiles and their kings and before the people of Israel' (v. 15).

Ananias knew better than to argue back or to ignore the call of God. He went—probably in fear and trembling, but he went—and when he met Saul he did not treat him as an enemy, but addressed him as 'Brother Saul' (v. 17).

Ananias was faithful. What would have happened if he hadn't kept the appointment that God had made for him—if he and Saul had never met?

What if he'd said, 'I'm too afraid to do this' or 'Perhaps it wasn't really God speaking, but just my imagination' or 'There's no way I'm going to have any contact with someone so opposed to our Christian views'?

Because Ananias met Saul, Saul met Jesus, and went on to become the apostle Paul, probably the most influential leader of the early Christian church.

Every day, people cross our path. How many of those seemingly chance encounters are divine appointments? Have you ever felt God's prompting to speak to someone, and yet something has held you back? You wonder how on earth to initiate a conversation. After all, you can hardly start off, 'Oh, by the way, I'm a Christian…'

Actually, God will help us in what we say, but ultimately it's nothing to do with how good we are at talking, or even how well we can present the case for Christianity. It's about being real, being honest, being humble and being available.

Divine appointments are not platforms for you to speak, but for God to speak through you and do his sovereign work. Then, just as with Saul, light breaks into darkness, hearts melt and lives are changed.

5 December

Is anybody looking for someone to star in one of those cough medicine advertisements? At the moment I would be ideal, as I am a living illustration of coldy misery.

Cough, cough, splutter, splutter, wheeze, wheeze. Look in the medical encyclopedia under 'coughs, colds and flu', and I'm sure I would be able to come up with 90 per cent of the symptoms.

- Scratchy throat that feels as if it's been scraped raw with the roughest grade of sandpaper.
- Wobbly and dizzy feelings: every time I try to get up, my head feels as if it's only just attached to my body and will float off at any moment like a balloon.
- Aches and pains: my legs hurt, my arms hurt, even my hands hurt.
- Runny nose: my stock of paper tissues is going down at an alarming rate, and the wastepaper basket is full to overflowing—again.
- Lack of appetite: I can barely swallow my cup of tea, let alone anything else.
- Headache.
- Coughs (like a hacksaw) and sneezes (frequent).

'You look terrible,' says my kind husband.

'Thanks,' I croak feebly. 'I feel terrible.'

Why did this have to happen today? I'm supposed to be driving down to the graduation of our oldest son's girlfriend.

'You're not going anywhere,' says my husband firmly.

'But…'

'You can't drive like that.'

'But…'

'No.'

He's right. My legs are like jelly.

'I'll phone and let them know you can't make it.'

'OK,' I say, unusually meekly.

It's not often I stay in bed, but today I can't think of any place I'd rather be.

Rome? Venice? Barcelona? No, today I'd trade the lot to be just where I am, snuggled up under the duvet. My body is in a battle against some germ or microbe that I can't even see, and yet it has the power to knock me sideways. I don't feel like myself at all.

It's strange how when we're ill even the most routine tasks can seem like mountains. Brushing my teeth is something I normally do almost without thinking, but today I can't face even the short distance to the sink on my weak wobbly legs.

I can't think straight, either. My husband pokes his head around the door. 'I'll get dinner. What would you like?' It's a simple enough question, but I can't make any kind of decision with a brain that feels like reconstituted putty. 'Anything. I don't mind.'

I just want to be left alone. In fact, I don't want to have to bother about anything—anything at all.

⁕

Symptoms are there for a reason. A runny nose and a fever tell us plainly that our body is sick and needs help to recover—perhaps by spending some time in bed, boosting our immune system with vitamins, or paying a visit to the doctor.

As a means of grabbing our attention, these outward signs that something is wrong generally work well, unless we have been living with the symptoms for so long that we fail to notice them any more. When warning signs go unheeded, serious disease, if left to its own devices, can build to a possibly fatal outcome.

Wake-up calls need to be taken seriously. Have you noticed

worrying symptoms in the world around us? It's hard not to, as newspapers and television programmes report escalating figures for violent crime, abortion, divorce and pornography, visible signs of a sick world crippled by a virulent disease that is slowly destroying it.

The first seeds of infection were planted when Adam and Eve turned away from God to follow their own path of disobedience, and this deadly inherited disease now affects all of us from the day of our birth to the day of our death.

It leaves us handicapped from the start, especially against an enemy less concerned with damaging our physical bodies than crippling hearts, minds, and souls: 'Do not fear those who kill the body but cannot kill the soul; rather fear him who can destroy both soul and body in hell' (Matthew 10:28, NRSV).

Satan's favourite tool is stealth warfare, a warfare that subtly invades our territory, taking ground inch by inch, until we find that we're wandering far outside our own defence lines, lonely, frightened and vulnerable, and an easy target for enemy fire, for wholesale infection.

When physical sickness strikes, our body is at war. As spiritual sickness has infected the world around us, we wage war against forces far more destructive than the most deadly bacteria.

Living on this planet, inflicting pain and destruction are things with which we are only too familiar. We know exactly how to play this game. Get bigger weapons than your enemy. If he hits you, hit him back—harder.

When we think of going into battle, our thoughts automatically turn to guns, explosives, nuclear weapons, biological and chemical warfare—instruments of war that will maim and kill.

So when we see what God expects us to use in our spiritual battles, it's a bit of a shock. In God's armoury we find no death-dealing weapons of mass destruction, but instead the belt of truth, the breastplate of righteousness, the shoes of the gospel of peace, the shield of faith, the helmet of salvation, and the sword of the Spirit, the word of God (Ephesians 6:14–17).

How can we possibly go into battle, where lives are at stake, equipped like this? It's hardly proper armour. Doesn't God realize how serious the situation is?

We would probably prefer boots with spurs on to shoes that proclaim the gospel of peace, but make no mistake, these spiritual weapons are powerful—if we learn to use them correctly.

One of the most effective weapons in our armoury is the word of God, the sword of the Spirit, used constantly by Jesus in situations such as his temptation in the wilderness (Matthew 4:1–11).

But even a sword is just a cumbersome piece of sharp metal if you put it into the hand of someone who doesn't know how to use it. To wield scripture effectively, we have to know it, really know it, and not just hope that even though we rarely read the Bible, some verse will magically pop into our head when we're in trouble.

Each part of this strange but highly effective armour has a special purpose that keeps us spiritually fit and well.

- We wear the belt of truth, against which Satan's lies are powerless.
- We cover ourselves with the breastplate of righteousness, to protect our vulnerable heart, so often an easy target.
- On our feet we wear the shoes of the gospel of peace, bringing news of a Saviour who has come into the world to bring an end to the warring in people's hearts—a peace that the world cannot give, but Jesus can.
- The shield of faith counteracts every attempt of the enemy to knock us off course, because we totally trust our living Lord.
- The helmet of salvation guards our mind, perhaps the weakest area of all, and reminds us that the accuser has no case against us, because when Jesus died on the cross our sins were covered by his blood.
- The sword of the Spirit cuts through the most impossible situations, when humanly speaking it seems that all is lost.

Being sick is not a desirable state of affairs. The enemy tries to distract our attention from what is happening by giving us a nicely furnished hospital room with all the latest mod cons, but it doesn't change the fact that we need to be healed and made whole, and that is beyond his power.

Although Satan pretends that he has our welfare at heart, all he can offer are shabby imitations and empty promises. Yes, he will give us what the world values—money, wealth and power—but he will destroy our souls in the process, for he is the great liar. For love, he substitutes empty lust; for truth, deception; for servanthood and equality as a child of God, slavery.

He can only give death, not life.

It is Jesus who brings new life to a sick and dying world. 'It is not the healthy who need a doctor, but the sick. I have not come to call the righteous, but sinners' (Mark 2:17).

We're already immunized, but there are countless others who are not. But it doesn't need to stay that way.

As we fight against the infection that sweeps over our land, we are not just soldiers. We have another role—paramedics. In our hearts we carry a precious antidote, one that will transform lives and make them not just well, but whole.

11 December

Crash! That's our letterbox—surely the noisiest in Exeter—and we've got a bumper load of Christmas cards from the sound of it! How I love hearing from old friends, catching up on what's happening in their lives—the highlights, the sadnesses.

As usual, one letter is particularly bulky, and I almost wilt even before I open it, because I know what's coming. What is it about this family? Somehow they seem to live on a whole different level from the rest of us.

Helen's got a promotion plus more money, and a new car. She's still heading up the children's work at church, and the Bible study group at her house is flourishing.

Sarah has just passed Grade 8 in the flute—with distinction.

Mike successfully passed his exams this summer—all As, and even a few A* grades.

Tom at university has just become President of the Christian Union—and he's only in his second year.

As for Mike senior, he's just published another in his best-selling series of Bible commentaries, added two more committees to an ever-increasing list, and been invited to speak in the Philippines.

Of course I'm not jealous.

I'm glad for them—they're our friends.

OK. You want the truth—how I really feel.

Very, very ordinary.

I want to pick up the phone and say, 'Yes, but tell us the bad news!'

✣

Have you ever wondered what it might have felt like to be one of the less well-known disciples—Judas, son of James, for example?

Imagine the scenario. Peter's been booked to speak at the church meeting, and the hall is packed. Everybody knows about Peter—he's one of the stars of the new church.

Peter's one of those guys everybody talks about—a larger-than-life character. You can hear people chatting excitedly as you thread your way to the front, virtually unnoticed.

'Did you hear about the way he stood up to the synagogue leaders that time? Told them nothing was going to stop him talking about Jesus, no matter how they threatened. That's Peter for you. Straight down the line. I'd have liked to see the look on those temple leaders' faces.'

And that's before you get on to the miracles, because of course that's another of Peter's credentials—he's been involved in a number of quite spectacular ones. You can hear that woman telling her friend, her voice high with excitement.

'Yes, it's true. My cousin told me. It was the lame man outside the Gate Beautiful—you know the one, he was always there. He's just like you and me now, two sturdy legs—why, he could run a mile on them!'

There's just one problem. Peter's not coming. Something's come up. And so Judas is here instead.

'Judas? Who's he?'

'Not the one who…?'

'No, that's the other one.'

Judas gets up to speak, feeling a little flattened, feeling the audience's disappointment that it's not Peter standing there.

It's not always easy to be alongside high-fliers. Saul certainly didn't find it so. Everything was fine when he was the king and David was just a shepherd boy, but then things changed.

He watched the shepherd boy become a gifted war leader.

He watched as his own servants applauded the young man.

He watched as it seemed that David stole Saul's place in the heart of his own son, Jonathan.

And he heard the women singing, 'Saul has slain his thousands, and David his tens of thousands' (1 Samuel 18:7) and something snapped.

What was Saul's reaction?

- Jealousy
- Anger
- Murderous thoughts

He couldn't accept that the anointing had passed to David, even though Samuel had already told Saul that the kingship no longer belonged to him (1 Samuel 13:13–14).

How different Jonathan was. In one sense, Jonathan had even more to lose. If David became king, it meant that Jonathan would have to give up the throne—his by right of succession.

Surely, Jonathan had every reason to try to thwart David. But he didn't. He was prepared to step aside because he recognized the hand of God upon his friend.

It takes a lot of character to be a Jonathan. When we see people looking to someone else rather than us to do the thing that we've always considered 'ours', it's hard to be gracious.

'I built the youth group from scratch… and now they're taking it away from me!'

'We've led this housegroup for years. Are you saying we haven't done a good job? Look at all the people we've helped.'

'But I always sing the solo in the Christmas service!'

It's a wise person who knows when to let go. Saul couldn't. His pride wouldn't let him, and maybe also his fear. Who would he be if he was no longer king? Who will we be if we're no longer heading up the prayer committee or overseeing the Sunday school?

Saul just could not accept that he needed to step down. 'My kingdom!' said his behaviour. He seemed to have totally forgotten that it was God who'd given him power in the first place.

In contrast, Jonathan was sensitive to God's Spirit. He saw the hand of God plainly on the young man David, and not only willingly gave up his own claim to the throne, but was also a constant support and encouragement to his friend. He knew it was time to hand the baton on.

Not all of us find it so simple. There's something in us that desperately wants to hang on to what we have, but that's actually the worst thing we can do.

God is not interested in half-measures. Passing the baton must be a deliberate decision on our part, not something we do because we feel we have no other option, or a last-minute decision that we've not really thought and prayed about.

It's all about our willingness to be less, but at the same time encouraging others to be more—not grudgingly, but wholeheartedly. And we will never be able to do that unless we ourselves let go, totally. No 'accidentally on purpose' fumbling the exchange, so that the next runner starts with a disadvantage. No trying to cling on: 'Well, of course that's not how I would do it!'

Think about the powerful ministry of John the Baptist where hundreds of people flocked to hear him preach, to repent of their sins and be baptized. If you were in his shoes, would you want to give it up? It would be more than understandable if he'd behaved badly when Jesus came along and stole the show. How did he react?

- With resignation? 'Well, all right then, I guess I'll just have to put up with it.'
- With jealousy? 'What's he got that I haven't?'
- With sulkiness? 'Well, in that case I'm not going to bother any more.'

John the Baptist did none of the above. He was full of joy when he saw Jesus in action. 'The friend who attends the bridegroom waits and listens for him, and is full of joy when he hears the bridegroom's voice. That joy is mine, and it is now complete. He must become greater; I must become less' (John 3:29–30).

When we see others forging ahead, we can do one of two things.

We can be passive, wasting our time wishing we were in their shoes, and just let them get on with it.

Or we can be active like John the Baptist and Jonathan, and get right behind them and what God is doing in their lives.

'Can we pray for you? Is there anything we can do to help? Go for it! We're with you in this—all the way!'

17 December

There's a lot of giggling coming from behind the scenes, and every now and then a mischievous little face peeps out from behind the blue curtain.

We sit on child-sized chairs in the school hall, where a Christmas tree festooned with homemade decorations stands, its dusky green branches almost touching the ceiling.

After some minutes, the curtain is at last pulled slowly back, and the children file on to the stage with some jostling for position. Little Hannah spots us sitting with her mum, Jo, and her face lights up. She waves, and Jo waves back.

One of the mums strikes a chord on the piano, and the children begin to sing rather self-consciously, aware that every eye is fixed on them. There's something magical about the sound of little children's voices, and there's not a rustle or a cleared throat from the audience—you could hear a pin drop in the crowded hall.

When they finish the song, we clap loudly, and everybody settles down for the next item, the well-loved nativity story, complete, of course, with the obligatory tea-towel headdresses.

One of the shepherds gets stage fright, and just stands there when it's his turn to speak, in spite of prompting from the teacher. 'We… must… go… to… Bethlehem…'

The innkeeper also has problems with his wife, who won't hold his arm as she's supposed to. In the end he gives up, and stands with arms folded on his own.

Hannah is a proud Mary, although at times she's rather careless with baby Jesus, holding him upside down until Joseph digs her sharply in the ribs to remind her how a mother should behave.

Jo's face beside me is glowing with pride. She may not be saying it in words, but she doesn't have to, as the way her whole attention is riveted on the little blue-clad figure of Mary, now vigorously rocking Jesus while the children sing the closing carol, 'Away in a Manger', gives her away. 'That's *my* little girl!'

There's a stage full of children, but as far as Jo is concerned, there is really only one, the beloved face that she picks out immediately from all the others. Jo watches Hannah intently, filled with pride at every movement that her daughter makes, and every word that she speaks.

❖

Do you know that God feels exactly the same way about us, and that he gives us the same quality of undivided attention? It's incredible that we should be so loved by God, the almighty creator of all things, but it is true.

When a new baby is born, the delighted parents marvel over every physical detail—the tiny curled fingers with their shell-shaped nails, that wonderful 'new baby' smell. Every milestone, no matter how small, is exclaimed over as a minor miracle.

'Did you see that smile?'

'Come to Mummy,' as the child wobbles towards a precarious first step.

'Say Dad, Dad, Dad, Dad…'

We don't mind the endless repetition involved. To us, it's enthralling, and we may even become baby bores because we cannot help boasting to our friends about little Johnny or Jane's latest achievement.

While others see only an average-looking child with a runny nose, we see our little one through rose-tinted spectacles. Never was there such a child! We are totally besotted.

As time passes, this first stage, when we are completely absorbed by the new little life in our care, moves on to a second stage. We no longer jump up to see what is wrong every time the baby cries—the novelty has worn off to some extent.

However, with God there seems to be no lessening in the enthusiasm with which he views us; there is still that sense of wonder and totally focused love, no matter where we are or what we are doing.

If you're feeling insignificant or lost in the crowd, you may sometimes wonder whether God can possibly be interested in you. The answer is a definite 'Yes—passionately'.

Fortunately, it's not a love that depends on what we've done, which is just as well, because if you are anything like me, you are far from perfect!

- I don't cope well with lack of sleep.
- I hate rotas.
- Church meetings often send me to sleep.
- I skip Deuteronomy (and Leviticus).
- I get PMT.

But God does not cease to love us when we (frequently) slip. Instead he speaks to us with words of encouragement, and sings over us with love (Zephaniah 3:17).

And where earthly parents may be too tired, or too busy, or just not observant enough to pick up on those times when we need extra encouragement, a shoulder to cry on, or even a stiff talking-to, God is always there for us.

God sees us as individuals, not just one of many.

'Look at Helen—look how she's learning to step out in faith. I'm so proud of her.'

'Look at Laura. I love it when she shares her disappointments with me.'

We are the cherished apple of his eye (Psalm 17:8), and he even knows exactly how many hairs are on our head (Matthew 10:30)—something that not even the most devoted parent will be able to tell you about their child!

He'd literally do anything for us. In fact, he already has.

He walked the long hard road to the cross because he loved someone who was totally, utterly special to him.

Chosen.

Beloved.

You!

Choices

It isn't what you know
But who you know,
And that is never more true
Than in our relationship
With God.

We can be experts in theology,
Plan talks with six suitably
Sanctified points structured to impress.
We can run our home and family
Like clockwork, following spiritual principles
To the very last detail.
But if God doesn't show up,
It's just an empty façade.

If he is there, it makes a difference,
The difference of an empty dark room
When you flick on a light switch
And everything is irradiated,
A leap from shadowy greyness
Into brilliant technicolour.

It's a mystery to me
Why some of us prefer rooms without light.
We know just where each wall ends,
The shape of the door and each window recess,
We can tell you the exact dimensions,
But without the light
It's just a box, an empty cube
And we cannot see our way.

Sticking close to the walls
We stumble in the darkness,
Never venturing out into that
Glorious open space in the middle.
How can we? If we did, it would mean
Leaving these safe boundaries,
And these are all we know.

There is a simple solution
For Light has come into our world,
So why choose to sit in darkness
When you could be
Walking,
Running,
Leaping
In the Light?

★ ★ ALSO BY CLARE BLAKE ★ ★

(Extra)Ordinary Women
Reflections for women on Bible-based living

Have you ever felt that women in the Bible were superstars, somehow extra specially blessed by God? And then looked at yourself…?

This book of down-to-earth Bible reflections is based around the central theme that all women are special in God's eyes. Relating scripture teaching to everyday experience, it shows how God has a special gifting for each of us, how we can turn to him when life doesn't make sense, and how to set about discovering his will for our lives.

Taking a fresh look at the stories of Sarah, Leah, Mary, and other Bible characters, we see how God looks beyond our failures and weaknesses to the women he has created us to be as we learn to follow him, step by step.

To him, each one of us is a 'one off' and in his eyes there are no 'ordinary' women—only 'extraordinary' women.

ISBN 1 84101 235 1   £6.99
Available from your local Christian bookshop or, in case of difficulty, direct from BRF using the order form on page 159.

★ ★ ALSO FROM BRF ★ ★

Women of the Word

Discovering the women of the Bible

Edited by Jackie Stead

As we read the Bible, it can be easy to overlook many of the women characters. While names such as Ruth and Elizabeth are familiar enough, what of the others, some of whom are not named at all? How much do we know about Abigail, Gomer and Hagar? About the Gentile woman who confronted Jesus, and the poor widow making her offering in the temple? What can we learn from these people and their experiences, to help us in our walk of faith?

This collection of Bible studies, written by a group of women writers, focuses on the lives of a host of female characters from both Old and New Testaments. First published in *Woman Alive* magazine as part of the 'Good Foundations' series, the studies unpack the original stories and show how these women can reach down the centuries and speak into our lives today.

ISBN 1 84101 425 7 £5.99
Available from your local Christian bookshop or, in case of difficulty, direct from BRF using the order form on page 159.

★ ★ ALSO FROM BRF ★ ★

Quiet Spaces

Prayer interludes for busy women

Patricia Wilson

The intimate relationship with God you've yearned for is well within your grasp, despite the chaos of juggling multiple roles, deadlines, and commitments. This book can help you to use even a few stray minutes as an opportunity for a 'prayer interlude', calming the mind and listening for God's still, small voice in the midst of the tumult around you.

Each 'prayer interlude', which can be completed in as little as five minutes, offers a calming passage from the Psalms, a prayer meditation, a thought from the words of Jesus, and an exercise to help readers as they go back into the busyness of the day.

ISBN 1 84101 339 0   £5.99
Available from your local Christian bookshop or, in case of difficulty, direct from BRF using the order form on page 159.

ORDER FORM					
REF	TITLE		PRICE	QTY	TOTAL
235 1	(Extra)Ordinary Women		£6.99		
425 7	Women of the Word		£5.99		
339 0	Quiet Spaces		£5.99		

POSTAGE AND PACKING CHARGES					
order value	UK	Europe	Surface	Air Mail	
£7.00 & under	£1.25	£3.00	£3.50	£5.50	
£7.01–£30.00	£2.25	£5.50	£6.50	£10.00	
Over £30.00	free	prices on request			

Postage and packing:

Donation:

Total enclosed:

Name _____ Account Number _____

Address _____

_____ Postcode _____

Telephone Number _____ Email _____

Payment by: ❏ Cheque ❏ Mastercard ❏ Visa ❏ Postal Order ❏ Switch

Card no. ☐☐☐☐ ☐☐☐☐ ☐☐☐☐ ☐☐☐☐

Expires ☐☐ ☐☐   Issue no. of Switch card ☐☐☐

Signature _____ Date _____

All orders must be accompanied by the appropriate payment.

Please send your completed order form to:
BRF, First Floor, Elsfield Hall, 15–17 Elsfield Way, Oxford OX2 8FG
Tel. 01865 319700 / Fax. 01865 319701 Email: enquiries@brf.org.uk

❏ Please send me further information about BRF publications.

Available from your local Christian bookshop.   BRF is a Registered Charity

Resourcing your spiritual journey

through...

- Bible reading notes
- Books for Advent & Lent
- Books for Bible study and prayer
- Books to resource those working with under 11s in school, church and at home
- Quiet days and retreats
- Training for primary teachers and children's leaders
- Godly Play
- Barnabas Live

For more information, visit the **brf** website at **www.brf.org.uk**

BRF is a Registered Charity